HEARTACHE

HEARTACHE

A healing place
for love
to grow

Ceil McLeod

Tyndale House
Publishers, Inc.
Wheaton, Illinois

Library of Congress Catalog
Card Number 78–64669

ISBN 0–8423–1407–5,
paper.

First printing, April 1979.

Printed in the United States
of America.

To my husband, Hugh,
whose courage, humor, and love
help me face the "breakers"
that would otherwise "beach" me.

To my friends
in The Saturday Club and The Robin,
for their helpful critiques.

CONTENTS

INTRODUCTION

After years of Midwest living, my husband, Hugh, and I
revisited the New England seacoast of our youth. With the
first whiff of salt air, we were home again. Daily we visited
the same nearby beach cove where we climbed among
slate-colored rocks or waded in chilly surf.

Each day the sea showed us a new mood. One day, sand
felt hot underfoot; sandpipers chased gentle waves.
Another, fog hugged ocean and shrouded rocks. Still
another, the ocean boiled a dull green, whipped up waves
that flung spray twenty feet into the air.

So it is with our lives. One day, ripples. Another,
hurricane waves. A sudden illness or loss, change of job or
location, and once quiet days fill with trouble.

No one runs toward experiences that create pain,
loneliness, difficulty. Rather, we take every precaution to
avoid such problems. But unless we choose the life of a
recluse, we cannot avoid complications, change, and times
of crisis. It is how we meet these interruptions in the flow of
living that really counts.

Life is seldom serene for long stretches of time. Life is
rather, as Paul Tournier says, "man in movement
continually undergoing change. The Bible shows man in his
living, in the midst of conflicts, of passions and forces which

determine his behavior. It shows him in his encounter which is personal beyond all others, his meeting with God."[1]

The same God who gave Noah specific answers (a dove with an olive branch, a rainbow) has creative ways of bringing an end to the storms in our lives. Edna Hong's findings from her research in suffering bear out what experience has taught me; namely, that "the greatest spiritual successes spring from the heart of suffering."[2]

Using vignettes of hurt both in my life and in the lives of others, I have here tried to show how God prepares us and how he carries us lovingly and creatively through trauma that seems unbearable at the time. Through him, such trauma gloriously hones us into the persons he planned us to be.

"I will not leave you comfortless," Jesus reassures us (John 14:18). He doesn't promise us endless days in a comfortable chair, but rather love and growth as we travel over bumps and washouts in life, whether on tricycle or in station wagon or wheelchair.

11

ONE
A CHILD'S PRAYERS

If the basis of peace is God, the secret of peace is trust.
John Benjamin Figgis

I was three years old. The floor by our brass bed was cold as
Mother, my brother Steve, and I knelt to pray. I snuggled
close to Mother. Steve wiggled, hiked up his pajama pants.
"Jesus, tender shepherd," we prayed in unison, "bless these
little lambs tonight. Keep us safe 'till morning light."
    A hug, tuck-in, lights out. I looked into dark shadows by
the door. It was all right. Jesus was there. I slept.
    Four years later, Jesus was still there though the room was
different, lit by a single bulb hanging from the ceiling.
Mother leaned close to my bed. Dr. Thurston held my wrist
with one hand, his watch in the other.
    "Thank God, Martha," I heard him say. "Your little girl
has weathered the crisis. She'll live." He blew his nose.
Mother's eyes spilled tears.
    Why all the concern, even if I had gasped for breath with
my combined illness of whooping cough and scarlet fever?
Jesus promised to keep me safe 'till morning light—he
always had. And there it was, just starting to come in the
window. Why do grownups worry so? I wondered.
    In those childhood days I saw Jesus one minute as a baby
in a manger, another as a shepherd with a lamb, and still
other times as a kind man kneeling in a garden to pray to his

Father, God. Mother told me that Jesus loved me; so did
our songs. I believed it.

One night when I was ten, Steve stopped abruptly after
"tender shepherd" in his prayer. "That prayer's kid stuff. I'm
going to say the 'Our Father' one," he said.
"All right," Mother agreed. So "the Lord's Prayer"
became our new nightly ritual. Much of it was fuzzy to me.
"Trespasses" were keep-out signs, weren't they? And
"hallowed" sounded like Halloween, but had nothing to do
with witches, Mother said. The bread part I understood and
the "Our Father" I really liked, but somehow "in heaven"
sounded such a long way away. But as long as "In Jesus'
name we pray" was there, I felt cared for and protected at
night just as with the simple shepherd prayer.

As with anything else new, we have to grow into prayer.
Those days I was slowly discovering who my heavenly
Father really was. Sunday school and Bible stories helped.
A crisis was coming into my life when I would need to know
my heavenly Father, not as someone in remote space, but as
a Father I could lean on. My earthly father was soon to
become a hazy figure. And most children accept God as a
loving Father in direct relation to their experience with the
love of an earthly father. As I grew in size, so did my Father
God grow in my understanding as I came to know him more
intimately.

TWO
GOOD-BYE, FATHER

Everybody believes divorce breaks up families. This is not so. The broken family is not the result of divorce; divorce is the result of the broken family. Paul W. Alexander

Our Father God—who is he and where is he? Those are big questions for little children to ponder. Jesus, born a little baby, was easier for me to comprehend. But I needed a relationship with our loving heavenly Father too.

As a little girl I had no idea cracks were developing in the fibre of my home, no knowledge it was built on quicksand from the beginning. Only years later did I discover the fatal flaw. Though my parents loved each other, they had ignored one of God's prime principles in marriage: "Be ye not unequally yoked together with unbelievers: for what fellowship hath righteousness with unrighteousness?" (2 Corinthians 6:14). Both partners in a marriage must come under the Lordship of Jesus Christ for a secure marriage. One partner *Christ-oriented* linked with one *materially* oriented will develop a see-saw relationship, hazardous to any marriage.

My mother, Martha Riggs, missionary daughter of Henry and Lucy Riggs, was joined in marriage to the son of a Boston banker in a hilltop Congregational Church in Grafton, Massachusetts. Diamonds sparkled on the groom's side, with worn Bibles more evident on the bride's. All agreed that Martha was radiantly beautiful, Max dashing.

No one then questioned the blending of their diverse backgrounds.

With the birth of a son, Stephen, one and a half years later, my parents' patterns of living came into conflict. Dad wanted more of the glamorous parties to which he was accustomed, while Mother sought a deeper church life. What had begun happily now began to deteriorate. The couple's concerned parents advised a move to Columbus, Ohio, where Max could settle into responsible family ways as a salesman under the training of his Uncle Will, who owned a shoe business.

Unfortunately this move failed to solve their problems. Instead, it deprived the children born of the marriage— Steve, Billy, and myself—of the nearness of our loving grandparents.

By the time I was five, we had moved again, to a Columbus suburb, one more step leading to Dad's eventually no longer living with us.

Quiet tree-shaded streets led from Worthington's main avenue with its old inn and shops. I was then a fragile child with a heart murmur, left over from an illness. Little did I guess that I would soon feel a deeper heartache, the result of my parents' divorce.

Our home, like others on Hartford Street, with its porch snug behind wisteria vines, was more comfortable than attractive. A tire swing hung under a shady apple tree. The rooms were big and square, showed no architectural imagination. I loved the songs, games, and stories of a nearby Sunday school, and with Mother's help was catching up on studies missed through illness over the past year. It was good to be strong enough to tag along after Steve and his gang. Sometimes he'd even help me get untangled when I got caught on the grape arbor.

Those were peaceful days—that is, except for my father's sporadic visits. Memories of earlier years when Dad came home regularly by streetcar began to fade. In a sense, my illness had aggravated my parents' troubles. Dad, Steve, and Billy, three years younger than I, moved out until my recovery. During that time Dad began to notice a young woman at his shoe store, but we kids heard nothing of this at the time.

We knew we had a father off somewhere, but he was a regular check, not a family figure. That is, until the Sunday that Mother announced, "Children, your father is coming to dinner. I want you to be on your best behavior and to mind your manners. No elbows on the table." Her glance lingered on Steve, who shrugged and went back to reading his Sunday school paper.

Good smells came from the kitchen. Roast pork crackled in the oven. A coconut cake sat on the kitchen counter (near enough to swipe some frosting). Mother had her best Italian cutwork cloth on the table. I arranged Mother's sterling with great care. Everything was prepared for a party. Why did Mother look like it was a funeral? She hadn't smiled all morning, even when I fixed a bowl of cosmos blossoms for the center of the table.

Long past the time when we were all slicked up and ready, we watched for Dad at the window. Finally his touring car jerked to a stop at the curb. Few men walked up our sidewalks these days, mailmen and milkmen mainly. Even so, we knew them better than this stranger, our own father.

"Hello, Max," Mother said.

"Hi, Dad," we chorused.

I watched Steve nervously tweak his cowlick. Neither of us knew what to do. After telling about school, what was left to say? I was glad when Mother called us to dinner.

"Your color is better, Martha," Dad stated casually.

"I'm feeling better, thank you."

"Ceil's gained weight, I see," he added.

For a second a half smile lighted Mother's face. "Oh, yes, the doctor is so pleased. No more being dragged to school by wagon. Ceil walks there now."

The coldness left Dad's eyes as he studied me. "I'm glad." I could almost remember the father who used to pick me up and twist one of my long curls around his finger. My eyes were getting blurry. His were too.

Steve's feet scuffled. His water glass swayed, crashed.
Mother swooped up his plate, pork and potatoes awash.
"Sorry, Mom."
Not a word from Dad. Now the stiffness was back.
Mother and Dad talked about relatives in the East. Just as I
noticed Dad's elbows on the table, Steve nudged me. We
looked knowingly at Mother. She flashed us a warning look.
The meal dragged on and on, way past the last crumb of
coconut cake.
"You children play a game while your father and I have a
talk," Mother said, warning in her voice.
Sliding doors closed behind them in the den. Steve and I
played checkers, losing track of turns while Billy watched.
Suddenly Steve stood up, scattering checker pieces.
Without a word he tore out the back door, around the
corner of the house. I tried to read to Billy, but neither of us
listened. Muffled voices behind doors went on and on. We
sat waiting. Something terrible must be happening behind
those doors. We were shut out and yet part of it.
The doors finally scraped open. Mother looked like a
worn paper doll. She dropped her handkerchief. It was
wrinkled and wet. Dad looked past us, his eyes angry, hands
clenched.
"Where's Steve?" he thundered. No answer, just a glance
at the door. He moved outside swiftly. More waiting. I stole
a look at Mother. She looked frightened, like I felt. I'd
never seen Daddy look that way before.
After a few minutes, we heard scuffling on the front
porch. Dad collared Steve and propelled him inside and up
the stairs, Steve kicking and twisting all the way. A door
slammed. Whacks followed in quick succession. Steve let
out a tortured yell. Then silence, which was worse. Mother's
arm pressed mine. Her shoulders shook. A tear splashed on
my forehead. I had never seen her cry before. Couldn't we
do something? When would it stop? Billy started to cry too.
Mother hugged us to her. We couldn't just stand there. I
broke away toward the stairs.
"No, Ceil, come back."

A door was flung open. Dad ran down the stairs. A final terrible look and he was gone—and with him the end of my safe little world.

Mother took the steps two at a time, Billy and I close behind. We all sat on the bed. No one talked. I was surprised to see sun streaming through the window. It no longer looked warm. There were shadows in the room that had never been there before, each one shaped like a big question mark. It was over and yet never really over. Such scenes tiptoe into the mind and hang there like dark cobwebs.

I can't remember ever hearing why Steve was punished. Maybe he needed it, but not in that way. Looking back, I can only guess this was the time when Dad insisted on a divorce and was angry because at that time Mother refused. God doesn't like divorce. Neither did Mother.

To my surprise, the next day began much like any other. As I let the dogs out the front door, I had an odd feeling I should be picking up branches after a storm.

Frying bacon smelled good. I glanced at Mother as she turned a crisp slice. She looked up, smiled, but I could still see hurt deep in her eyes. Who would help her? Whenever I had a hurt or a problem, she usually fixed it for me with a Band-Aid, glue, or maybe just a hug. But this was different. Maybe God could do something, but what? This was beyond my usual "God bless Mother and Daddy and make me a good girl." If I'd only known about God's promise, "I am sufficient for all your needs," it would have helped. It would be years before I found out how real and personal God can be to us in trouble.

Just at this time I discovered the book *Little Women* by Louisa M. Alcott. Beth, Meg, Jo, and Amy became just as real to me as my best friend Harriet Kemp. Didn't they live in a fatherless home (he had gone to war) like us and didn't Marmee shower love on her children as our mother did on us? And couldn't we make a ballgown for me out of our lace curtains if I should need one someday? I was sure of it.

Later on, I read another favorite book, *The Secret Garden*

by Frances Hodgson Burnett, and there I read of a beautiful refuge from an angry world, a garden where beautiful events took place. I too needed such a perfect little world away from the storm. I looked again at my picture of Jesus talking to God in a garden. God hung moss on trees and made butterflies out of caterpillars, didn't he? Of course he was part of gardens.

A skinny girl with long curls and dresses with matching bloomers, I made an overgrown vacant lot my garden. Harriet and I lettered a layered piece of wood with the rather crooked words "Treasure Trail." We had to enter between prickly overgrown hedges. We pressed matching keys, tied around our necks, to a low tree branch to unlock the trail. We tiptoed in. (It's easy to frighten little garden creatures.) On our way we gathered pink and white hollyhock flower ladies and acorn tea cups and saucers. These were soon arranged on deep velvet moss between roots of a giant elm. All in readiness, we sat cross-legged, waiting for the orchestral tune-up. Crickets tilted willowslip violins. Elves tumbled down from accordian undersides of mushrooms. Fairies no bigger than our smallest finger, arrayed in gowns to match their wild rose houses, danced lively jetés on the velvet. Faster and faster they twirled until only color patterns flowed before our dazzled eyes. Then with cymbal clash it was over. Tiny figures scattered. Only a songbird broke the silence. We left quickly, still hearing lovely sounds in our ears. We never told anyone of our garden; it would all vanish with grown-up laughter.

Of course little girls grow up and grownups put away childish things, or they should. However, when I make dresses for our granddaughter's dolls, I'm not quite sure which of us enjoys make-believe more.

I know now that children facing ugliness they neither understand nor can control need some outlet. Mine was a mysterious garden which fed my imagination.

Already shy, I retreated and became still more shy, especially around men. I believe that little girls learn to trust men by what they see in their father.

I saw God reflected in Mother and in my maternal grandparents, but didn't see God reflected in my father. In addition, as Dad became less evident in my life, I felt a new burden. I believed that if I had been more deserving of Dad's love, he wouldn't have left us. In some vague way, I felt I had failed him. But I hid this deep inside me. Only when grown did I understand how foolish this thinking was.

How different it would have been if we had felt free to ask Mother, "Doesn't Daddy still love us?"

She might have answered, "Yes, of course he does. Nothing that happens between your father and me will change our love for you children. Your father misses you terribly and wishes he could have you with him."

That would have opened the way for us to ask, "Why was he so mean to Steve?"

"He was angry today, but not at you and not really at Steve; he is unhappy because of his problem. I know you find this hard to understand. It's hard for all of us." With such a discussion, we could have faced the hurt together.

That Sunday is the only time I remember seeing Dad really angry. He had been a bright boy, spoiled somewhat by wealthy parents who were loving and cultured, but not deeply Bible-oriented. When denied his desire for divorce, Dad's inner resources failed him.

Unfortunately not all children pass tenderly from childhood to adulthood. But even though the discord of my parents hurt us, we were fortunate in that we knew we were loved by both Mother and Dad.

Not long ago I talked to a young man who spends his off-hours playing ball with deprived young people. When he talked to them about drawing close to God as heavenly Father, they turned away in disgust. Puzzled, he sought out Dr. Bob Smith, world lecturer and a former professor at Bethel College, to find out how to teach the love of a heavenly Father to young people with poor concepts of their earthly fathers.

"I followed Dr. Bob's suggestion to ask them how they wished their own fathers would treat them," he said. "One

said, 'I wish my old man would quit slapping me around.'
Another said, 'Wish mine would get me some of the stuff I
need instead of spending all we get on booze.' And still
another, 'If only he'd talk to me, not just swear at me.'

"It was no wonder they didn't associate love with *father*,"
he continued. "I explained how God provides for all our
needs, never rips us off, how he always feels our hurts, and
how he loves us even when we disappoint him. That cleared
the air. They were eager to know someone like that."

All kids need a loving father. My relationship with God
began to grow, but I also needed to see love demonstrated
by another human being to help build my image of God as
Father.

My mother's brother, Uncle Alfred, treated me with the
same loving consideration he did his own children
whenever I visited them in Grafton, Massachusetts. From
him I learned the warmth of God as Father by adoption in
preparation for the time years later when I would be
adopted into the royal family as God's daughter.

God can ease our hurt and loneliness and provide a
healing place for love to grow as his love is made evident
and meaningful by others.

THREE
GOD AND GRANDPARENTS

Is your Christianity ancient history or current events?
Samuel M. Shoemaker

A child needs to know that God is real. Religious trappings
mean little unless the child sees God alive in someone. God
was alive in my mother's mother, Grandmother Riggs.
Through her I came to know that God could be trusted to
deliver what he promised. In turn, I wanted to be trusted
both by God and Grandmother. We all became a working
team, not in an ethereal somewhere, but at Grandmother's
house. God's ground rules didn't change from day to day,
nor did Grandmother's.

The summer I was twelve, Steve and I were sent ahead of
Mother and Billy to my grandparents in Grafton,
Massachusetts, for the summer. Mother stayed behind to
sell our Ohio home and arrange for our move east.

Together with my cousins, I explored the yard, past rows
of bearded irises that waved their heads beside a white
picket fence. Then we trooped down a sloping side yard
across from what was once our family shoe factory, but now
was used as a garage with apartments overhead. Flower beds
laid out like zinnia petals were already bright with blooms.
Over behind the big house, rows of gooseberry bushes hid a
chicken pen and, best of all, frolicking kittens, gray and
fuzzy and begging to be held.

Our arms full of kittens, we raced up steep back stairs through the kitchen, where tantalizing roast beef was already browning in an old wood-burning stove. Spiraling back stairs took us to the upper bedrooms, down a dark corridor over toward Uncle Alfred's quarters, through a Victorian bedroom to the best room of all. It was a large screened porch lined with double-decker bunks where I was to sleep with my cousins. Even the old morris chair still stood in its accustomed place. All, all was the same. Too happy for words, I bounced on my cot. This had to be the loveliest place in the world, full of hugs and God, cousins and kittens, and room to stretch and grow.

This was the world where I became a whole person. Here problems were taken to God, who found answers to everything. No lonely corners exist in a house alive with cousins. Even rainy days became glorious adventures with cupboards full of books and old magazines, costumes of faraway days (complete with hoop skirts) on the third floor, and on the second a huge closet filled with silks, ribbons, and buttons for thimbled fingers.

Men lived here too: Grampa with his funny mustache that went up and down when he talked; and Uncle Alfred, who talked mostly with smiling eyes that said I was special to him. Being accepted into Uncle Alfred's family as just one of his kids took away some of the hurt and confusion of my feeling rejected by my father.

All the Christian wall plaques and Sunday lectures in the world are as nothing compared to a home where children feel lovingly accepted and comfortable in discussing God's ways.

Mornings at Grandmother's were worth getting up for. Grampa would light a fire in the dining room fireplace. Then he and the current tiger cat warmed themselves while Grandmother brought in johnnycake from the oven. After Grampa gave thanks, Grandmother's smile moved from one to another of us, telling us she was glad we were gathered together to eat of God's abundance. Breakfast was full of chatter and laughter. After the last bite, we filed into the

front parlor. Steve and I raced for seats on the horsehair
sofa next to a tall curio cabinet. On one particular day, Steve
was allowed to select an object from the cabinet, a leftover
from our grandparents' days as missionaries to the Sioux
Indians at Santee Mission, Nebraska. Then
Grandmother would tell a story about that item.

But first, Grampa read a chapter from the Bible. Then we
knelt on the wide board floor with its carpet pieces. While
Grampa prayed, Steve and I were tempted to gaze at his
tilted black shoes with puffed toes. We knew he was missing
some toes, but weren't sure how it had happened.

"In Jesus' name we ask it," Grampa concluded.

"Now for the story," we chorused.

"All right. What is your choice, Steve?" Grandmother
asked.

As we knew he would, Steve picked the war club, an
egg-shaped stone with sharp points, slung on a wooden
handle covered with deerskin.

We sat motionless, soon transported from Grandmother's
parlor to a rough cabin in wilderness country. We marveled
at her true story of a confrontation with an angry Indian
chief who ended up asking Grandmother to teach him and
his daughter to read. The two later became fine Christian
leaders.

I stared at Grandmother. How could such a fragile lady
be that brave, I wondered.

"Honey, some day you'll be as terrified as I was." She
always seemed to know my thoughts. "But just hang on to
God, and you'll find strength you never knew you had. He'll
not only keep you safe, but he'll give you a way to turn the
whole experience into his glory. You'll find that love casts
out fear, and his love is perfect."

I looked over at Steve, big for thirteen. His eyes shone.
Compared to him, I was always such a sissy. But maybe God
could make me brave, that is, if it was to do something for
him. Tomorrow I'd pick the story that went with the pin
cushion that Grandmother's Indian girls had made out of
beads.

Later Grandmother handed us an icy pitcher of lemonade and some cups. "Here, children. Take this down to the swing where it's cool." She knew the double-seated swing with its latticed backs was our favorite summer spot, nestled as it was under the tall elm in the deep backyard.

The swing moved gently. A breeze ruffled damp curls on my forehead. This was the loveliest place in the world. If only Mother and Billy were here, it would be completely heaven. Then an ugly thought crossed my mind. They were closing and selling our Ohio home. Nothing had been said about where we would live next. It would be wonderful if it could be Grafton. Then these perfect days would never end. But it might be near Grandmother Holmes, Dad's mother, in the city of Newton, Massachusetts. Though I loved her, the thought of a city home bothered me. It was better not to think about it, to just drift with the days—swimming at Kiddieville, visiting Aunt Mary, and playing in Aunt Kathrina's attic full of antique doll furniture.

The weeks passed quickly.

In a corner of the dining room, Auntie Mary had a tall built-in white cupboard jammed with Sunday school supplies. These included a tiny-scaled ark filled with animals and a replica of the ark of the covenant. Each facsimile had its own Bible story, and Aunt Mary told them with her whole heart. We looked forward to rainy days and the opening of the cabinet.

The Bible became real to us not only through stories of missionary days and recountings of Bible events, but even more through everyday happenings in which Grandmother and Grandfather showed their trust and dependence on God. Because he was real to them, he became real to us.

Grandmother not only trusted God, but she trusted me too. When we are trusted that way, it's almost impossible to let a loved one down. I was Grandmother's errand girl. In a drawer in the dining buffet lay her black leather purse. Inside that was a smaller black silk purse which usually held no more than coins and a dollar or two, enough for my

errands. Sometimes I was sent to the A & P with its pickle
crocks and prune bins. I was usually offered a sample while
waiting for baking powder or coffee beans. Or I might be
sent across the town common to the meat market with its
damp floor littered with shavings.

Grandmother's money was different from my father's
checks. Grandmother's money all belonged to God. Many
times I had heard Grampa and Grandmother discuss a need.
After prayers she usually said something like, "It's all right,
Henry, God will provide as he always has." And he did. It
didn't matter that Uncle Lewis, who owned an oil well in
Texas, often supplied a new oil furnace or a new enamel
icebox when the leaky one gave out. Uncle Lewis was just
helping distribute God's wealth.

Mother and Billy arrived July 2. As golden days passed, I
became sure Grafton would be our new home. I gained
weight on Grandmother's cooking and developed
swimming muscles playing water tag with cousin Maida and
Steve.

This summer must never end! But it did—and worse, the
news came that we were to live in Newton, Massachusetts, a
few blocks from Grandmother Holmes' stately mansion.

"Why do we have to live there?" I fumed.

"Because if we live there, your grandmother will see that
you children have every advantage," Mother said. I saw a
worried look in her eyes before she turned away. "Newton
has fine schools. Your father grew up there. You can have
dancing lessons and go to concerts."

"I'd rather go berrying and swimming at Kiddieville.
Please let us stay here," I begged.

Now Mother's eyes filled with tears. I knew she loved
Grafton too. There must be another reason to make us
leave Grafton.

When we moved into the snug brown-shingled house
that September in Newton, I found out the reason. It had a
terrible name—*divorce*. The word reminded me of divided
force and it was just that. That's the way I felt—cut up and
cut off. As Mother explained the terms of divorce, we were

to live with her in Newton except for occasional visits with Dad, who was remarrying and moving to New Jersey. Seeing our father would be easier, she assured us, if we lived close to Grandmother Holmes. Further, Newton offered superior financial and cultural advantages compared to "small town" Grafton.

We sensed Mother was doing what she thought was best for us. It was all settled. We must pick up the pieces as Mother was already doing. There was nothing else we could do.

FOUR
RENDEZVOUS WITH GOD

*There is no surprise more wonderful than the surprise of being
loved; it is God's finger on man's shoulder.* Charles Morgan

I had experienced a father's love in Uncle Alfred. I felt the
reality of God in Grandmother Riggs' hugs, stories, and
trust. But I needed to know who I personally was to God.
For our rendezvous, God selected the ocean at Boothbay
Harbor, Maine.

The move to Newton brought me into a new and closer
relationship with Grandmother Holmes, my father's
mother. At thirteen I was already four inches taller than
Grandmother. Her dominant conversation and compelling
blue eyes made me feel unsure of myself, though I knew
she loved me and I loved her. I sensed as I looked around
her handsome home that I needed some grooming to fit
into her cultural and social ways.

In Grandmother's spacious dining room, a Venetian glass
fishbowl stood on a wrought-iron base before a window
looking out on woods and brook below. Fan-tail fish swam
in graceful circles in the bowl. I watched one float to the
front, then dip her iridescent tangerine tail toward me as
though saying, "What a stiff, colorless creature *you* are."

I stared back at her. No fair; I'm on dry land (though even
in clouds of chiffon I could never bend and twirl like her).
Still, I thought, she can only go around and around in her

circular world. I can plunge into a wave's crest, arch up on its swell, skim high, then crash into the soft foam around me. Goldfish are prisoners in glass.

But in a way I was a prisoner too. For Grandmother Holmes planned to make a lady of me if it killed us both. After school, she pinned and fitted dresses and slips on me. I'm sure she never realized that those slips made of fine lawn edged with French lace flounces removed from old petticoats made me the laughingstock of my peers. The other girls were lucky—they could wear their plain white slips. With my long hair pulled into a bun and my mid-calf dresses, I thought I looked like a skinny librarian, but Grandmother approved.

On the other hand, Mother thought of me as her little girl. She liked my hair in stiff long curls, and my lanky body in short yoked dresses with ribbons dangling from the shoulder. Either way I felt like somebody's imitation. If only grown-ups would let us be free to grow inside as our arms and legs grow on the outside! I often wondered just who I really was.

I found out later that most adolescents ask, "Who am I—will I find my place in the world—will I feel out of place—will I be accepted or rejected by my fellow classmates?" It seems to me Dr. Paul Tournier grasps that feeling when he says, "Even in early infancy the great thing—on which one's whole future life will depend—is the dawning consciousness of oneself as a person. This process depends very largely upon the respect which the child's parents, brothers, and sisters have for his personal place: if not a room, at least a small corner he can call his own, where he can leave an unfinished game without someone coming and tidying it away: if not a cupboard, at least a drawer in which he can keep his treasures."[3]

I had a place, a lovely rosy-chintz bedroom which I shared with my mother, but no hideaway private place. This plus the charade of trying to be Grandmother's young lady one moment and Mother's little girl another, plus the feeling of rejection by my father, made me unsure just who and what I was.

That is, until my visit along with Mother and Grandmother Holmes to Newagon Inn at Boothbay Harbor the following summer. Newagon Inn was even lovelier than I remembered from a visit two years earlier. I stopped to listen to the crash of the surf, to watch a seagull soar out of sight. I sighed. The call of the ocean must wait until after lunch with Mother and Grandmother Holmes. I quickly smoothed my hair, straightened my skirt. Grandmother liked everything just so. They both glanced up, smiled as I slipped into my chair in the chintz-draped dining room.

"What will you have as an appetizer, apricot nectar or fruit cup?" Grandmother asked.

I was ravenous, all the way to my toes. But after three courses I was stuffed. Two more were still coming, plus endless discussion of concerts, exhibits, and side-trips. I wiggled impatiently. What a waste of a glorious day at the shore. Finally Grandmother pushed back her chair.

"How about a walk around the grounds," she suggested. I saw Mother's sympathetic glance.

"Oh, Grandmother, couldn't we do that before dinner? I'd so love to put on my bathing suit and sunbathe on the rocks. Then I could meet you at the pool later."

Grandmother bit her lip, considered. "I suppose so, if you'll keep away from the edge. Maybe it would be a good idea for us to have a rest, Martha, after that long train and boat ride."

"Whee!" Shoes and skirt were peeled off, bathing suit slipped on. Free at last. I raced over pampered green lawns toward beckoning rocks. My hair slapped at my eyes as I scrambled over boulders, searched caves for secrets, found bits of driftwood and crabs trapped at tide's turn. Glorious! I stomped seaweed, listened for its pop. Leaving far behind the world of "do this, do that, be ladylike," I climbed even higher. Far below waves pounded, sending up a fine mist.

By now my bathing cap bulged with sea treasures, toes rubbed on sandpaper-like barnacles, only to slip later over slithery green moss. Then I saw my hiding place. Under an overhang of rock lay a hollowed-out pool of foaming saltwater left behind at tide's ebb. I edged my body down into the sun-warmed crevice until smooth rock embraced me. It fit me like a sneaker, even to the sloped back. I was tucked away; only God knew where. Far above, a piece of sky blinded me with hot sunshine. I could hear my heart beat in time with the rhythm of the surf. My eyes closed.

Now it was as though my body floated, my spirit in tune with sea and rocks. God seemed close. For the first time I realized God had made me, just as he had made the mighty rocks. In his image, somebody had said. Sun-warmed, rock-supported, sheltered, I felt I was about to begin a new life.

"God," I breathed, "is this what I really am, free yet safe because I am a soul made by you? You know all about me, don't you, God?"

A glorious peace wrapped around me. Time stopped, until a cloud covered the sun and my pool felt chilly. It must be late. Grabbing my towel, I scurried over rocks, once again at the mercy of grown-ups and their rules. But now I was me and God's too, not just theirs.

I believe each of us at some time needs to feel God's breath on us, a quickening when we recognize God as our Creator and discover we can have fellowship with him. It helps to get away alone in a lovely setting, but it could happen anywhere. The important thing is that it occur before we become imprisoned in a cooped-up, frustrated existence. We can experience this in the branches of a shade tree, bobbing in a sailboat, or on a hilltop, any place where we feel the warmth of God's love. What is important is not so much the specific place, but personal relationship with God.

We need, I believe, to expose our children to spots of beauty and also to loose the leash enough so they feel God's freedom within a context of caring. I'm glad it happened to me.

FIVE
NO ONE BUT GOD

*Right is right, even if everyone is against it; and wrong is wrong,
even if everyone is for it.* William Penn

The discovery on Maine's coast that I was a person
important in God's sight gave me a security that helped me
through high school and college. I continued those days to
try to please both Mother and my Grandmother Holmes.
But there were times when I was torn by conflict. Mother
approved church activities, while Grandmother bought me
French dresses, loaned me her emerald ring, and
encouraged occasional dates with the yachting crowd.

Mother died very suddenly, during February of my
sophomore year at Simmons College, just two years after
the death of my Grandmother Holmes. Cut off from advice
by Grandfather Riggs' death and Grandmother Riggs'
serious illness, and now unmoored from Mother's gentle
anchoring love, I was adrift and fearful. Temptation pressed
in, while there seemed to be no one to guide or correct me.
That is, no one but God. After the double hurts of a
summer's broken romance and my loneliness for Mother,
God seemed faraway, as though he didn't care. This left me
vulnerable as never before.

Driving uphill to the Sunapee Lodge brought a flood of
memories. Howie, at the wheel, was friendly but distant.
We had both changed since last summer's romantic days.

After Mother's death, the breaking of our relationship had been traumatic.

"You're the only one of the old crowd to return this summer, Ceil," Howie said. "Barb Brindle from Colby Junior College is your roommate. She's been here a week already."

"Will we still be in the little house?"

"Yup."

Neither of us spoke as the old car climbed past birch groves glinting white in sunshine. What would this summer be like, I wondered, being once more in the little house with its two double rooms for college waitresses, with Howie's room and the bath up front. I suspected Howie was thinking the same thoughts. This was the first time we had seen each other since that awful night in Boston when he said, "See you around sometime," and left without a backward look. I glanced at his profile, boyish chin, and those incredible black lashes shading dark eyes that had often searched my secret thoughts. His tight grip on the wheel belied his casual air. So last summer still haunted him too. It seemed silly to pretend it had never happened.

The road blurred. I was once again running over the meadow with Howie, stopping breathless at a split rail fence while he helped me over. Birch leaves rustled a welcome. Howie grinned as I gathered a bunch of daisies. Arm in arm we straddled boulders, headed for a stand of white pines ahead. I breathed pine-scented air, ducked prickly branches. It was cool and dark. Our feet scarcely touched the soft needled carpet. Only our breathing broke the silence.

A shaft of light created a wavy gold pattern at our feet. As one, we craned our necks upward toward the slit of sun above. God seemed close. Howie's arms folded around me, his kiss gentle. For both of us love was as new and shining as the beam of light.

The slowing of the car startled my thoughts. Howie burst in on my reverie. "Here it is. Lake Sunapee." Far below us blue water shimmered, broken only by a wooded island.

"It's as beautiful as ever," I sighed. "Some things don't change."

Howie glanced over at me, for once off guard. Now it was my turn to look away. We slowed for the entrance to the Inn. "I'll take your things up while you check in with Mother."

"Thanks for everything, Howie." I was glad that I also could sound nonchalant.

Mrs. Bronson was as gracious as I remembered her. She smiled, said, "Welcome back, Ceil." She handed me my room key and listed serving hours and station in the dining room. As I turned to leave, she pressed her hand on my shoulder. "Ceil, I'm so sorry about your mother's death. We all miss her. I'm grateful for her visit here with us last summer." (Mrs. Bronson had been a friend of my mother's in college.) "I expect this has been a difficult year for you." I couldn't face the kindness in her eyes. "Thank you . . . Yes, it has." How silly that my chin still trembled four months after Mother's death. The tenderness in Mrs. Bronson's eyes was worse than Howie's matter-of-factness.

"Please let me know if I can help in any way," she added.

I tried to smile back, but it came out more like a grimace. I blinked furiously to keep back tears. "Thanks," I managed, then fled as tears fell.

I was glad no one was around as I hurried towards our quarters. I needed to be alone to slough off memories and make a new beginning. The room was orderly, my roommate's shoes coupled in a row, clothes tucked on her side of the closet. I arranged pajamas and underwear in the empty bottom drawer. It might be all right. At least I would be making some new friends. Barb must still be on duty.

It was getting warmer by the minute. I laid out my new flesh colored bathing suit with its bare back and tangerine edge. Any funds I had always went into a new suit. For me, summer was swimming.

Voices and laughter broke the hot stillness. Steps sounded on the path. A petite girl with dark curls and

laughing eyes bounded in. "Hi," she said. "I'm Barb
Brindle. Glad you finally arrived."
   "Hi, I'm Ceil Holmes. Hope you don't mind my stashing
my things."
   "'Course not. Sooner the better." She handed me a box.
"Here's your uniform. Hope it fits you better than mine did.
It almost hit my ankles. Why don't you try it on and then
let's go for a swim. I see you're ready for one."
   At 5'6" and size 12 my uniform fit me perfectly. Barb
groaned, "You don't need to do a thing. How lucky can you
be!"
   Lucky! Barb might have to shorten skirts, but I doubted
she faced family deaths and broken romantic affairs, by the
look of her dimples and confident smile.
   Barb was good company. She knew kids with summer
cottages on the lake. We were soon double-dating in a fast
crowd, unlike anything I'd known before. I'd always been
shy in high school, judging guys by Mother's standards,
afraid to trust men much after my parents' divorce. Couples
at these parties would vanish for hours. Most drank heavily.
I felt conspicuous sipping Coke. After two nights in a row
with Barb's friends, I saw Howie eye me as I started out the
door.
   "Do you really dig that crowd?" he asked.
   "Sure. Why not?" I retorted. Why should he care? But I
was secretly glad he seemed to, and also glad he didn't go
with the bunch. He'd be as uncomfortable as I.
   One night Barb fixed me up with Stew, a handsome guy
who had expressed a special interest in me. I hesitated, then
agreed to go out with him. We double-dated with Barb and
her fellow.
   We sped dangerously up mountain roads. I looked at
Stew. His skin was greasy, eyes hard under slicked-back
hair. It was his hands that worried me. His fingers seemed
restless, full of tension. By contrast Howie's hands were
clean and firm. Whatever was I doing with a boy like Stew?
Mother certainly wouldn't like him. I didn't much either.
But it was a date.

It was dark by the time we pulled into Barrington, our destination for this evening, and all we saw of the town was bars and the like. The hours dragged on. I longed to leave. On the way home I tried to sleep, but the sounds in the back made it impossible. Besides I kept seeing Mother's face, looking hurt. I glanced at my watch when we stopped at a traffic light. Two o'clock. The car finally pulled into the parking lot by our hotel.

Stew released the steering wheel, grabbed me. His hard cheek pushed mine down toward the seat. "Let me go," I yelled, lurched toward the door. Shocked, he sat bolt upright. The door opened and I was gone, tearing up the hill. I knew he wouldn't dare follow, but I trembled until I pushed the door closed behind me.

I tried to sleep, but lay frozen with fear, the whole ugly night pouring past in review. Barb slipped in hours later. I pretended to be asleep. She soon was.

The next day I decided to take a good, long walk. The dirt road felt good to my feet. I passed a farmhouse. A brilliant green field fragrant with clover rose to my right. Rocks clustered at the top. I climbed slowly, my tears making it hard to see hummocks of grass.

"What's wrong with me, God?" I shouted into the clear air. "I feel like I'm a battlefront. It's beautiful here, but somehow it's all spoiled. Nothing's the same, no Mother, no Howie. It used to be easy to be good, because I couldn't bear to hurt Mother. Now there's no one to care. I can do anything, even go with that gang. But I feel dirty when I'm with them. They don't really care about each other, just bedroom stuff and drinking. What do you really want for me—am I to be a lonely old Puritan curled up reading books? I've tried that."

I climbed up on a flat rock. Tears of self-pity splashed down my face. The rock felt hard and rough; so was life, I thought. Far below, Lake Sunapee sparkled, untouched by my problems. I looked far out where fluffed clouds were playing tag. Everywhere I looked the world was bursting with color, but for me it might as well have been raining.

"Isn't there anything for me, anybody but that stupid gang?"

Suddenly I saw the kids as God saw them, the waste of all he gives us. "Yes, God, I was part of that and I'm sorry. No, I don't want that, but don't you have something for me that's good?" My throat ached. "I can't go it alone, with no one to care where I go or what I do. Oh, God, I'm an awfully big overgrown girl to be crying here for her mother. What's wrong with me? Do you really care?"

It was as though someone pressed my shoulders and hugged me. "You know I love you, Ceil," God seemed to be saying. "Both your mother and I care what you do. You've been dependent on your mother too long. It's time you start being yourself, your real self. Just try it. I'll help you all the way. After all, I am your heavenly Father." The words sang in the air.

The hurt was all gone. I lay down, closed my eyes. "God, I love you," I breathed and then slept peacefully.

It was cool now, the sun behind clouds when a strange sound wakened me. *Crunch.* I sat up, startled into alertness. Barely four feet away a cow slobbered grass, her brown eyes watching me. Three huge animals, horns glinting, lumbered in behind her. One rolled its eyes until only white showed; another pawed the earth. They were closing in around me. My red shorts! Bulls!

I dodged the first, almost bumped into the one with those rolling eyes, ducked around the horns of another. Panic took over. I raced toward the farmhouse far below. I tripped, heard a bellow close at hand. On I ran, and on, until my lungs refused to supply me more air.

Two farmers, pitchforks in hands, stood below staring.

"Help," I screamed between gasps. "Can you tell me which of these cows are bulls?"

They all but doubled up laughing.

Now more embarrassed than frightened, I dared to look up the hill. Only a quiet herd of cattle met my eye. "Oh . . . I . . . I was asleep on the rocks. When I woke, they were all around me."

"It's all right, lady. We meet city slickers all the time. Them cows is right friendly."

I hurried off. Then the last few days began to strike me funny. I chuckled. The world was still right side up and God was in control. I was the one who had been out of step. It was time I grew up and learned to make right decisions. I discovered later that all of us have times when we need to get alone with God to get back on course. I wish I could say I always followed his ways from then on. But at least the direction of seeking to walk with God was established, and I knew I could count on him for my mooring post wherever I was from then on.

Howie was on the front steps as I sauntered up. "Hi, Ceil," he called. I could see warm glints in his brown eyes. "How about a swim this evening, over to the island and back?"

"I'd like that."

Back in my room, I smoothed burn ointment on my forehead. "Thanks, God. I'll try to let you take over. It works better that way, doesn't it?"

SIX
MY TUG OF WAR

*There is a time we must firmly choose the course we will follow,
or the relentless drift of events will make the decision.*
Herbert V. Prochnow

Just a year prior to my first summer at Lake Sunapee, I paid
my first visit to my father, stepmother, and five-year-old
stepsister, Betsy, in New Jersey. Only then did I realize how
cloistered I'd been. I felt gauche and Victorian at their
high-ball parties, and I'm sure I didn't add much to their
gaiety.

Dad was kind, my stepmother friendly, but I sensed they
didn't quite know what to do with a "dropped-from-the-
past" Bible-belt daughter.

The situation, though sometimes strained, certainly
wasn't grim. Dad's summer cottage on Lake Glenwild was a
lovely spot to get reacquainted, particularly with Betsy,
whom I'd only seen briefly at Christmas gatherings at
Grandmother Holmes' home. Betsy was lively fun. We
gathered blueberries, swam and sunned on the rocks, and
used a doll bottle to nurse a newborn mouse Betsy found.

Most of all, however, I loved swimming across to the
island or past a row of small cottages. My favorite swim took
me past a green cottage where a young man was one day
repairing his dock.

About the same time I slowed down my crawl, he
lowered his saw. His friendly "Hi" brought me to the dock.

Faced with his college-business aura, his muscular build, and the fatal combination of blue eyes and strong chin, I was tongue-tied. As we enjoyed long swims to the island and back in the next days, we found out much about each other. Soon we were double-dating with his sister and my brother, Steve. Just out of high school and seven years his junior, I was flattered by his attention. Fearful of being dropped, I tried to appear sophisticated, ordered my first Tom Collins.

Ours was an occasional, vacation romance with months and miles (Boston to East Orange, New Jersey) between dates. We were both dating others in addition to our infrequent times together. Hugh's honesty and kindness drew me to him. Though my mother never met him, she liked what she saw in his picture on my desk. Expecting to see her recoil in shock, I said, "But, Mother, he drinks and smokes."

"That's not the most important thing in the world," she replied.

My Simmons College classmates thought him dashing and handsome and magnanimously offered to take him off my hands if I decided in favor of another fellow I was also dating then. Eventually I realized I loved Hugh and ditched the other guy. Only later did I discover that Hugh also broke off another relationship for ours, with a beautiful concert artist.

We married in July 1938. It was a joyous marriage. We traveled together throughout the South as he taught sales schools for a large manufacturing company. Our joy seemed complete with the birth of our daughter, Gail, three years later.

But after a time the same flaw that had broken my mother's marriage caused lightning flashes in our own. Cocktail parties were routine in Hugh's sales world, as well as in his home background. Heavy drinking and dirty stories at sales gatherings made me uncomfortable. I felt loved and cherished, but at times such entertaining blasted away at our togetherness.

On Memorial Day, 1946, battlefields of war seemed only

a blur of history. Peonies tossed their petals against the gray
of our split rail fence in Reading, Pennsylvania. Clumps of
daisies dotted country fields beyond. Like many other
dining tables in America that day, ours groaned under
molded salads, thin sliced ham, and a crock of bubbling
baked beans. I checked the table once more, straightened a
leaning iris. *Let this be a holiday to remember, dear God,* I
prayed.

Outside, watermelons bobbed in ice-filled tubs. A chilled
beer keg stood under a leafy catalpa. I grimaced. Why did
the sight of a harmless keg of beer bother me so? After all,
it was only a beverage like punch or coffee. But I couldn't
reason away the panicky feeling. Instead of a keg, in my
mind's eye I saw my father's frequent glass of beer. What
part had it played in my parents' marriage breakup? Would
it crack mine open too?

A car door slammed. The sun glinted on Hugh's blond
hair. He smiled as he hurried past me to greet our guests.
After eight years of marriage, that smile still melted me.
The fear pushed back, I rushed to join him.

Soon cars lined the country lane. Hot sun beat down on
bare arms and shoulders of young women in rainbow-hued
dresses. We chatted as I ladled lemonade from our cut glass
punch bowl. Hugh was surrounded with guests under the
shade tree, filling beer mugs.

Hours passed. No one seemed to want to come indoors.
Finally I called to Hugh, "How about getting the gang in for
dinner?"

"Oh, let's wait a while longer, until it cools a bit more," he
answered.

My lips formed a grim line. What about my dinner?
Salads, in spite of being revived in the refrigerator, already
looked wilted in the heat. From the corner of my eye I saw
two fellows roll out a fresh keg of beer. More beer! Surely
that wasn't necessary. Some in the group already looked
glassy-eyed. A chorus of "Daisy" started up. I tried to catch
Hugh's eye, but he was too busy filling mugs.

I joined some girls trading recipes, but found little to say.

Anger now took over. How dare Hugh ruin supper by prolonging the drinking! Why was it I seemed so often to play the role of spoilsport while Hugh was the generous host?

Forty minutes later the air was cooler, but I wasn't. I maneuvered through the noisy crowd around Hugh until I stood close enough to hiss in his ear, "Either we eat now or else."

"OK, OK." He could see I meant business. "Drink up. We're being called in to supper." With that he led the way.

Now I busied myself filling platters, wiped at a blob of raspberry Jello on embroidered tablecloth. It only smudged worse. Laughter drifted in from the back fence. Couples balanced plates as they ignored picnic tables to mount high, precarious seats. A crash, more laughter, the tinkle of broken china. Oh dear, was that the Wedgwood or our everyday dishes?

The party seemed out of control. I felt ready to scream even as I mouthed pleasantries. Evening came.

"Come on, honey. Some of the guests are leaving," Hugh called.

Honey, I thought. How dare he!

We smiled and waved good-bye in a pretense of perfect unanimity. As the last car pulled away, I stomped inside. I washed dishes while Hugh lugged in furniture.

With order restored, I climbed wearily into bed. I needed no rockets' red glare to know a battle was brewing.

"Nice party, humm?" Hugh stated into icy silence. A sniff was his only answer.

"What's the matter with you?"

"What do you think? Your beer ruined everything."

"Everyone had a good time. If you had relaxed and not been so dead serious, you would have too. Forget it. I'm bushed. Let's go to sleep."

He was soon snoring while I lay staring at the ceiling. I was glad our daughter, Gail, was on an overnight. I didn't want her to feel insecure as I had years ago over my parents' disagreements.

It's odd, I thought, how one quarrel can spoil days of peace and love. Certainly no wife ever had a more loving husband than I. Any time I needed help, he was there. We were in tune on most everything: raising the children, decorating the house, churchgoing, saving for college. Was there something the matter with me that I got so upset over a little hilarity and a few broken dishes easily replaced? Why couldn't I slip into the expected groove of hostess for a successful business executive?

Deep underneath I knew why. How much drinking did it take to break up a marriage? The least sign of slurred speech or unsteadiness made me fear the worst. In addition, I had an uneasy sense of guilt. In our early dates I'd appeared to go along with Hugh's enjoyment of nightclub life. That was a natural part of his world from the time he joined the DKE Fraternity at Colgate University, which I'd heard at times laughingly referred to as the Dirty Drinking Dkes.

I'd gulped down Tom Collinses as though they were lemonade, even overdone it a bit to the point of being silly at times. But underneath, I'd been afraid to let Hugh know how I really felt, that I'd far rather hear a symphony than Benny Goodman, skip highballs for ice cream. During my college days, I used to stare at drunks stumbling back and forth at the subway as some kind of dreadful freak. My family had never even served wine, and I was well aware of what the Bible said about drunkenness. If only I'd been honest with Hugh in the beginning—but I hated to sound mid-Victorian and I couldn't risk losing him. Somehow he never seemed to mind my background; that is, unless I turned preachy following a drinking spree.

Fortunately such parties were infrequent, usually triggered by business affairs. No father shared more with his daughter than Hugh. She adored him, and why not? He rushed from executive meetings to watch Gail recite. He put on shepherd's clothing for church pageants. He lavished me with flowers and lovely clothes and encouraged my community activities.

Why, then, when married to America's dream husband, this worry about occasional heavy drinking? I felt torn between the world's "drink and be merry" and God's "moderation in all things."

I tried to find a middle road, but often felt like a piece of elastic stretched so tight I might break. Climbing a catwalk with God is precarious. I began to have fainting spells, which occurred after an occasion of what seemed to me overdrinking. It became a tug of war between my love for Hugh with his social ways and God's orders.

Our see-saw problem continued to frustrate me in years to come. But God knew our difficulty all along. Not all problems evaporate with a snap of the fingers, much as we wish they might. Some take years, and perhaps a spiritual change in outlook, for a permanent solution. Years later our "bottleneck" broke.

SEVEN
WHEN LOVE IS SHARED

God helps us to do what we can, and endure what we must, even in the darkest hour. But more, he wants to teach us that there are no rainbows without storm clouds and there are no diamonds without heavy pressure and enormous heat. W. T. Purkiser

Winter came and went. The woebegone country house we had purchased now sparkled with ruffled curtains, dainty flowered wallpaper, and wide-board waxed floors. Gail, now six, practiced acrobatic stunts on the split rail fence. Long walks by the Schuylkill River brought discoveries of wild flowers and plump raspberries.

At the same time, Hugh's business prospered. We all reveled in our country surroundings, but one disappointment clouded our days. Ever since Gail's birth we had been anxious for more children. Though a series of surgeries had vastly improved my health, it still did nothing to change that situation.

We had almost given up hope. But in February I became suspicious, then sure after seeing a doctor. I could scarcely wait to tell Hugh the good news. I was expecting at last. Our guest room was soon transformed into a nursery.

However, our first joy was short-lived. Cramps and staining put me to bed, as did drugs used to protect the pregnancy. I lay in bed four months, knitting and sewing and reading to Gail while housekeepers came and went. By the last month, my doctor encouraged us that all was well. Love mounted for the precious life within.

My water broke two weeks early. In Reading Hospital's lobby I gave Gail a big hug. "It won't be long, honey, before you have a sister or brother." Her eyes danced.

The hours dragged past. Hugh took Gail home and returned to wait. With dawn just breaking, I was wheeled into the delivery room, my pains close together and sharp. I could take in the room with its bustle of white-clad nurses since I had asked that I be given no anesthetic.

Five hours later I heard my name called. "Ceil, Ceil, can you hear me?" The voice echoed from far away. Once more, closer this time, "Ceil."

My eyes opened. I was aware of a hospital bed, intense quiet, then nothing but the saddest, darkest eyes I have ever seen. Never moving, they filled the room with a compassion that reached inside my soul, shouting, "I care."

Dr. Kotzen, my skillful Jewish pediatrician, wanted terribly to tell me something . . . something.

As my eyes closed, I was back in the delivery room, purposely wakeful to be first to see my baby. Suddenly a violent push brought blessed relief from pain. I saw my doctor lift a baby to the arm of a waiting nurse. A tremulous cry interrupted the clatter. Then silence. It was terrible. I raised my head in time to see my baby carried to a table. A nurse quickly blocked my view. In the deathly silence I called out, "What's the matter? Is something wrong with my baby?"

Instantly an anesthetic cone was pressed over my face. They weren't supposed to do that. My cries stopped in a sickening flood of ether. I dropped into nothingness . . . nothingness . . .

"Ceil."

I remembered the dark eyes. "Yes, Dr. Kotzen."

"There is something I must tell you."

"About my baby?"

"Yes, about your son. Sometimes nature tries to warn us that something is wrong, but the drugs we gave you held your baby to term."

"Yes, I know," I interrupted, "but what is wrong? Please tell me. I can face anything if my baby just lives."

"The best surgeon in Philadelphia is operating on your baby right now, doing all that can be done. Your son was born with his lower abdomen laid open, kidneys, and other organs not connected. It is very serious. Even if he lives through this, there will be more operations later and we can't be sure that he will walk or even eat normally. I want you to pray that your baby will die!"

Hardly believing the horror of those words, I exploded, "Never! That would be like murdering my own child."

His eyes never left my face as he leaned closer, holding my hand. "Ceil, you just don't understand the heartbreak ahead for you and for him if he lives. Nineteen days ago a baby was born in Philadelphia with one eye in the middle of his forehead. So far he is still living!"

"But my baby isn't a freak! I saw his beautiful little head and his legs kicking. We'll do everything for him if it takes all we have."

"Oh, my dear, you have no idea of the future. Thank God for your daughter, Gail. I still beg you to pray that this baby won't live." With this last remark he squeezed my hand and turned wearily toward the door.

As a nurse gave me a hypo, I drifted away from the sharp pain.

Later I wakened to my husband's gentle kiss, our tears mingling wordlessly.

"Tell me, how is our poor little one?"

"They operated for three hours. They were amazed that he stood it so well. They had to connect his stomach and kidneys, but couldn't finish it all."

The following day I held our baby—we called him Bruce—devouring his 7 lbs. 2 oz. of beauty, his eyes blue and wide open, chin rounded like his sister's, blond hair. How perfect he looked. How could there be so much wrong? He moved and cuddled in my arms.

"Oh, dear Lord, please watch over our little one. You

know how we love him and he's so beautiful. How can I pray what they tell me? Please, dear heavenly Father, do what is best for him."

As days passed, my bundle grew lighter, his little face lost the rounded look, and he was less alert. On the sixth day, they wheeled me to him in a small room in the children's wing where the head nurse cared for him as though he were her own.

The next day he was very sick, little twitches and shudders passing over him, later becoming convulsions. This day I was to go home. How could I leave him? Again I prayed at the tiny bed, my tears dropping on his little face. Did God really want him back . . . and why? I wondered.

When I arrived home that late September afternoon, our catalpa trees were brilliant in green-tipped gold. I was amazed at the riotous color and warmth of the sunshine after the quiet struggle of the hospital.

With Gail in my arms, our cocker puppy licking my face, and my husband's smile of welcome, I suddenly realized how good it was to be home. Life does go on. Beauty and warmth don't stop with sorrow.

As I sat on the terrace listening to happy chatter, the phone rang. When my husband returned, his carefully composed face told me all. "Our little one went back to be with God, darling, just five minutes ago, peacefully in his sleep."

Somehow the sun felt cold; dry leaves rattled. One dropped in our path as we went quietly into the house.

"Honey, I hate to mention it, but they think an autopsy might help in future cases. What do you think?" Hugh asked gently.

"They can't hurt Bruce now. Why shouldn't they, if it will help another?" I answered sadly.

Late the next morning, our young obstetrician drove up the lane. As I hurried to the door, my heart went out to him. His face showed the difficulty of his errand.

"Please sit down, Mrs. McLeod, while I tell you our findings." It was all highly technical, but it seemed that far

more was wrong than they had first thought. No feeding
except intravenous ones entered Bruce's stomach. I
listened, the words blurring, until he stopped, hesitant to
go on.

"You see, what we thought were part of a boy's sex organs
were really a girl's ovaries. You had a daughter, not a son."

"Oh, no," I murmured stupidly, "our Bruce couldn't have
been a girl!"

"Yes, he was. In the baby's open abdomen, these parts are
so tiny that it was difficult to tell the gender."

After the first shock I felt a strange sort of relief. A voice
seemed to say, "Your baby was just loaned to you by God.
You never even knew it was a little girl. Now she is with
him, whole and beautiful, no longer yours on loan but a
precious addition to the kingdom of heaven."

Three weeks passed. Slim once again in a cocoa wool
dress, holding Gail's hand, I walked slowly with my family
toward the gloomy portico of Holy Cross Church. There
seemed no reason to hurry. Dry leaves crunched under
foot, lifeless and shriveled.

As we mounted the steps, two slight figures left a
chattering group of teenagers, shyly stopping us.

"May we talk to you a minute?" the girls asked after
introducing themselves as Suzanne and Alice.

"Why, of course. What is it?" Hugh answered.

"Well, we've been asking for a Sunday evening youth
group. Everyone tells us it has been tried, but won't work
because we're too busy. Honestly, we will come and we'll do
all the work, but we have to have a sponsor. Won't you be
our leaders?"

There was no dodging the appeal in their eyes. Startled, I
queried, "But why us? We've had no experience with
teenagers. Our Gail here is only six."

"That doesn't matter. You're the kind we want. Won't
you please believe in us? No one else does," Alice pleaded.

"For heaven's sake, why shouldn't you have a Sunday
youth group if you want it?" I said. Hugh nodded. "I
certainly loved mine when I was your age. Look, we'll see

what this is all about and report to you tonight."
Exchanging smiles, the girls rushed off as the bell tolled.
Hugh looked at me. "Are you serious about this?"
"I don't know, but those kids deserve a chance. Oh,
darling, do you suppose God filled us with all this love for
our baby, took her away, and then meant us to use it for
these young people? Do you suppose it's all part of his
plan?"
"Maybe so. If you're game, I am. Let's go in. We're late
now."
A year later, the basement of our church echoed with
applause as curtains flapped shut and floodlights dimmed.
Easing back in my prompter's seat backstage, I straightened
my tight maternity dress. A sudden kick startled me.
Suddenly I was no longer alone. My husband's warm
hand pressed my shoulder while Suzanne, stately in brown
silk, hurried toward us. "We have a little gift for you, Mr.
and Mrs. McLeod."
Behind her, Alice, clothed in gold taffeta, held out a slim
square package. The rest of the cast crowded around. "We
don't really know how to thank you. When no one else
believed in us, you offered to help us start this youth
group."
As I unwrapped a heavy silver tray garlanded in
remembrance pattern, Suzanne's soft brown eyes and
Alice's honest blue ones brimmed with love. Alice
continued, "We've learned so much about Christ this year in
our Sunday evenings together."
"So have we." Hugh grinned back at them.
Taking my eyes from the eager faces reflected in the
gleaming tray, I looked toward them. "It was you who gave
us the greatest gift. The love for our lost baby lay heavy on
our hearts. You received this love, turning it into a precious
adventure in faith. We not only learned to love you, but we
drew closer to God because of you. He turned our sorrow
into joy, and in extra measure is giving another baby to us.
Before we go home, let's sing that wonderful old song,
'Blessed Be the Tie That Binds.'"

As their young voices rose in song, tears filled my eyes.
The little one within moved as though wanting to be
counted too.

The next June, God, in his loving way, sent us our son,
Hugh, who always seemed God's special replacement.

God never wastes anything. When he fills us with love, he
gives us a way to use that love. Love is meant to be shared.
Love stored unused becomes dried like a wizened prune.
But love grows as it is given away.

EIGHT
ILLUSIONS OF HAPPINESS

My most cherished possession I wish I could leave you is my faith in Jesus Christ, for with him and nothing else you can be happy, but without him and with all else you'll never be happy.
Patrick Henry

As one year followed the next, Hugh's business prospered. He earned the distinction of Life Membership in his firm's Hundred Club, an honor awarded for being a top national sales manager ten years in a row. With this success came moves to Cleveland, Chicago, Indianapolis. As the children grew, we were active in PTA, church, and community. Those were glamorous years of decorating new homes, entertaining, and participating with our children in Little League or Brownies.

Being of the kind of New England stock that longs to root deeply, each time we pulled up stakes and moved into a new home on another treeless lot I felt as though a part of myself had been left behind. I grieved for rose gardens begun, bulbs planted and never seen to bloom. I sewed drapes for each new home, until it seemed I had curtained the land.

But with new plantings, new friends, and new activities, life continued. I accepted the expression "Bloom where you are" as a sort of motto and joined groups as though my life depended on them.

At the same time I continued trying to entertain for Hugh, with as many as thirty-five guests stashed at tables everywhere but the bathroom. But along with the business entertaining, the drinking hovered like a time bomb ready to destroy the joy of gracious hospitality.

With our daughter a senior in high school and our son in third grade, we should have been experts in family raising and social climbing. But it wasn't working out as we had planned. Our church life was more social than spiritual, parties seemed increasingly out of hand, and business was slow.

Outwardly all appeared well, but inwardly I began to feel something was vaguely wrong both with the world and myself. What had happened to my bluebird of happiness?

Where was the sustaining faith, both for our children and ourselves, we expected from our church? Instead, at that time our son seemed to make excuses about going to Sunday school, unlike him. I began to read his lessons and discovered passages that would seem to breed doubt, not faith, in a child. Added to this, I read a magazine survey that concluded that young people were more apt to lose their faith at religion-oriented colleges than at secular ones. (I have since found the reverse often to be true when a college stresses a strong personal relationship with Jesus.) These observations shook the ramparts of a faith I had counted on, and betrayed cracks.

Not that I doubted God, but he seemed distant. I became aware of dust on my Bible. Without realizing it, our version of the American success story had created a wedge that threatened our relationship with God.

Meanwhile, I served on a Washington Township School Board committee investigation of prestigious secret social clubs that appeared to have dubious value. The deeper we dug, the dirtier the facts we uncovered (such as members being required to steal and commit sexual acts). Suddenly our gentle Indianapolis suburb with its redbud trees and twisting brook seemed a Sodom or Gomorrah.

Not only was it a rude awakening to discover I could count little on institutions like school, church, and college

to instill morality and faith in our children, but at the same
time I had to face up to the insufficiency of my own faith.
All this overwhelmed me. But even more, I was appalled by
the frightening results of alcohol I saw around me. Drinking
loomed more deadly than bullets.

God knew I would be taking this journey. He had
prepared me many years back. Each time I battled with
myself against the effects of alcohol, God was saying,
"There is a better way—I will show it to you—trust me." In
Chicago he brought me into a courtroom to testify against
an alcoholic mother who lived next to us and was incapable
of caring for her young daughter. In Cleveland he showed
me the evil of a business manager (he worked next to my
husband) who persuaded sales personnel to start lunch with
midmorning martinis. God introduced me to a talented
New Orleans salesman who in an alcoholic stupor leaped to
his death from a hotel window.

Holiday gatherings are too often ruined by exotic-shaped
bottles tied in tinsel. "Holiday cheer," it's called. Others
know it differently. How many family Christmases are
shattered by the maudlin office party leading to a
"hung-over" Santa Claus in the home? How many lives are
eventually destroyed by the open bar that precedes most
business affairs, I wondered. Certainly there are thousands
of discreet and dignified social drinkers. But which of these
will become statistics in the future? By the neighborhoods
in which I have lived, I would judge the hazards to be
frightening.

At this time I read a statement in our local newspaper,
written by an Episcopal priest: "My goal in life is to
reconcile people to God. Day after day I counsel people
whose lives have been ruined through alcohol. If
unknowingly by serving a drink to a single person
chemically unable to handle it I lead that person into this
kind of tragedy, I would be going against God. Therefore, I
choose to refrain from ever serving alcoholic beverages."

I now laid aside novels, lugged home stacks of religious

books from the library. I confined my entertaining to iced tea luncheons. Office Christmas parties became punch and cookie affairs, much to the disgust of many employees.

Over the years, as many social drinkers tend to do, we had succumbed to the pattern of a cocktail or two before dinner. It took a crisis to break up this pattern. Hugh was transferred to St. Paul, Minnesota, while, as usual, I stayed behind to sell our home. In that interminable six-month period, only one area of my life improved. On Hugh's next weekend visit home, I finally dared to tell him about it.

"You know, honey," I began, "this has been one of the worst times for me. You know all of us miss you terribly. But there is one thing I really like."

I swallowed. Could I really tell him? Could I risk hurting him, maybe even losing him?

"Go on."

"You know, honey, when dinner is ready it's nice just to sit down and enjoy it. I never have to wait around for a cocktail that I really don't want. Dinner tastes better, we have more time to talk together, and life is more peaceful."

Hugh looked stunned. I hated to hurt him. I plunged on.

"I'm sorry, honey, but this is sort of a freedom from drinking and all the problems that go with it. I like it."

Hugh just stared, sat as though frozen. I looked away, blinked back tears. I'd done it. Then I felt his hand press mine. "Guess I never really understood." His words were so low I could hardly hear. He drew me into his arms.

Relief flooded me. I'd finally said it and he understood. The wonder of it. After all those years of fear, pretending, and resentment, it seemed so simple. Now I could begin to be the self God wanted me to be and let Hugh be himself. "Let go and let God!" That isn't a bad slogan Alcoholics Anonymous uses. My tug of war with God over alcohol was over. It was a release for us both; Hugh no longer pressed me to join him for a cocktail.

During those days of facing up to the alcohol problem and the insufficiency of my faith, I had become a seeker. And Christ promises that as we seek him, we will find him.

However, I had no idea then that my search would take five years, including months of pain following a spinal fusion, and eventually involve not only a move to St. Paul but to a church different from any we had known before.

Over the Christmas holidays we sold our house, loaded our things into a huge moving van bound for St. Paul, and bought a snug gray house on a hill. We were on our way to become part of Minnesota, but far more important, part of God's family.

NINE
CALVARY ROAD

I was made to see, again and again, that God and my soul were
friends by his blood; yea, I saw that the justice of God and my
sinful soul could embrace and kiss each other, through his blood.
John Bunyan

Palm Sunday, 1964, was chilly in St. Paul, Minnesota. That
first year we had visited all the likely churches on our list as
we sought to draw closer to God. Yet somehow we found
them wanting. We began to wonder if the lack was actually
in ourselves. While visiting, we heard highly trained choirs,
shook friendly hands, and found cultural variety. But God
still seemed distant, not close to us in the pew. We were
spectators of the panorama of God, not part of his family.
And it was no longer enough to be part of a sanctimonious
pageant when I longed to be lighted from within. But how?

There were times when I felt some Christians held
freshly picked violets, dewy and fragrant, while I clutched a
limp plastic fascimile that smelled like stale kitchen.

Palms arched over the church platform on Palm Sunday
morning at Calvary Baptist Church. We sat close to the
front. Choir voices soared in hallelujahs. The pastor's deep
voice told of Christ astride a donkey, riding in triumph into
Jerusalem.

How could things change so radically in just the few days
that followed that ride? Those who cheered on Palm
Sunday scattered. From a triumphant figure, Jesus became a

condemned man, bruised and beaten, now on his way to the cross.

As I eased into a fresh position in my stiff pew, I felt myself transported back 2,000 years to Jerusalem. I stood on a balcony, looking down a winding, cobbled street. Even while I listened to sounds of a waking city, hot sun already brushed my face. Preparations were being made for three executions on Golgotha: two thieves and a troublemaker named Jesus who had turned over money tables at the Temple, gathered crowds on hillsides, told the people strange stories. Birds flew away from the sounds of nails hammered into wood.

A holiday mood exploded in Jerusalem. All around me, families with baskets over their arms strolled in the street. The fragrance of freshly baked bread mingled with salted fish and sharp cheese. Children sprawled on stone balconies, waiting for the coming procession. Women in bright headgear leaned from windows to catch a glimpse of this Jesus who called himself the Savior of the world, but couldn't even save himself from crucifixion with thieves.

I heard shouts, then the dull sound of a dragged cross. As the crowd drew closer, taunts filled the air. "Ha, the King stumbles. See, he sweats like any of us."

I leaned forward to see the approaching figure. Was this just another pageant, a parade of a suffering Jesus not so unlike the Christmas pageants of my youth when I stood robed in white, mouthing "Lo, a star shines in the east"? Just another time when I tried to be like Jesus, only to fail once more? I was weary with failure.

As the procession slowed, dust settled, revealing Jesus bent under a heavy cross. He drew closer. Now I could see dirt stains on the hem of his robe. Suddenly I felt the years of inner loneliness like a lead weight within me. Could Jesus take that weight from me?

But how could he? He had more than he could bear himself. He paused to shift the weight of his awkward cross. Veins bulged on his wrists as he clenched the crosspiece.

He strained up the steep hill, then suddenly stumbled, rested his weight on one knee. Blood spurted from a gash on his forehead as the cross slid to a rest. Flies buzzed around his head.

I stared, unable to speak. Jesus blinked in the bright sun, glanced up momentarily. His eyes met mine. Love deeper than any I had ever known flowed like a life current toward me. Even in his suffering, he cares about mine, I thought. O Jesus, you are real and you do care.

I wanted to cry out, "Help him," but couldn't move my lips.

A man edged from the crowd, thrust one shoulder under the cross. Jesus stretched his sore back, then plodded once more on his way.

My thoughts were interrupted by the pastor's voice. The scene he described had changed now to the hill of three crosses. I glanced toward my husband and son. Both sat motionless beside me, eyes glued to three crosses over the platform.

In that moment all three of us stood at Golgotha.[4]

We shuddered at the terrible sound as nails pierced bone while Jesus' hands and feet were nailed to rough boards, at the pain on his face as his body hung in position. Sun beat relentlessly down on the sagging figure. Then his gentle voice, "I thirst." We saw the Master's dry lips open for a vinegar-drenched rag. His eyes sought the heavens. "It is finished," he said. And darkness fell. The earth trembled in its bowels and people fled. The lonely figure hung there.

For the first time we knew why this terrible death took place. It was for us. It was not just a story of something that took place 2,000 years ago. It was real, and it is real today. He died that we might live. Live how? Live in him.

I was startled to see tears in my husband's eyes, his hands knotted in anguish. He, too, stood at the foot of the cross that moment. We watched Jesus die, and it was terrible and beautiful. For it was God's gift to us. What greater gift could he give. I glanced toward my son. His blue eyes shone and he smiled back tenderly. To give up one's son! "Oh, God," I breathed, "thank you for your gift. How can I be worthy of such giving?"

The last hymn note faded. Pastor Frykholm stood below the platform, eyes tightly closed. "Are there any here for whom I may pray? Are there any here who would accept Christ's gift of eternal life, his promise that 'as many as received him, to them gave he power to become the sons of God, even to them that believe on his name'?" (John 1:12).

Both my husband and son raised their hands. I simply could not lift mine, and soon the service ended.

I was the last to come to Christ. My pride broke more slowly than that of my husband and son. I had been so sure that the religious background of my youth made me somehow more pure than others. I can guess now what Jesus would have said to me. "You knew in your Grandmother Riggs a woman deeply filled with my Spirit. I spoke to you often, but you turned away. Does this make you holier than those who never saw me in others?"

When Pastor Frykholm asked the question again two weeks later, I felt my arm rise, without quite knowing why. *Pray for me please,* my heart demanded. *I want the gift you offer.* I wanted to be God's daughter, no longer an outsider.

My long loneliness for God was over. With the acceptance of Jesus' offer of himself on the cross came not only an inner filling, a cleansing, but a new direction and vision. Only those who have gone from despair to hope can know this "fountain of life" feeling. Rebirth is the only word that expresses it.

I believe that loneliness for God is the greatest anguish a person can suffer, whether caused by alienation from God or by being a believer who lacks total commitment. Such loneliness sharpens each sorrow and diminishes each joy.

No grief so far experienced approaches this ache for God; not the breaking apart of my childhood home, the death of my mother, the loss of a longed-for baby, fear of alcohol, pain of spinal illness. These all hurt and needed to be hurdled. But the hollow God places inside us can only be filled with Jesus. As long as this hollow lies empty, we suffer with soul cancer. I believe that no one can be a totally fulfilled person until that one has met Christ personally at the cross. With Christ at the center, all the jagged pieces of our lives smoothed out. The cross became a turning point for each of us. Not only were we flooded with new joy and a fresh look at the world around us, but Christ became an oasis where we drank deeply after our desert trek. I joined a Bible study and visited a Christian Women's Club where I listened in amazement to the stories of others who had found this relationship too. I had no idea how many pilgrims had been searching while I searched. In our loneliness it is easy to believe we are the only ones suffering. Spiritual emptiness is not the sort of thing one shouts about at a street corner.

Now when I wasn't dashing to a meeting, I had my nose buried in books—C. S. Lewis, Catherine Marshall, Dr. Paul Tournier. Where had they been all my life?

My husband went to Christian Business Men's luncheons and early morning Bible studies.

For our son Hugh, Sunday became the frosting on his cake. Besides Sunday school and church, both morning and night, he found time to put on some afternoon programs at nursing homes with his gang. And this was the boy who had objected to Sunday school just a few short years earlier!

I'm sure we bored friends and family. We wanted everyone to take a flying leap at the cross, and we shared our new knowledge as though the Bible had just come off the press for the first time. New Christians can be a menace. After all, it took us some forty to fifty years to knock on the door of the house of God's family. Not everyone around us was traveling the same route, or was in the same state of readiness. As some we witnessed to reared back in self-defense, we came to realize that God gives each of us the right to accept or reject his way. No one can be pushed into the kingdom, and we better not try. But how do we find the seekers? This isn't easy, we learned.

There was a new direction now in our community

activities. Not only did we want to help others, we wanted to tell them of Jesus. I became a hospital volunteer, eventually president of the auxiliary, where I could push patients to therapy and share the Good News. It wasn't long before I found a dormant talent, previously never suspected, that of writing. When you yearn to do something for God, as I longed to tell what I now knew of him, God gives you a way. He led me to Christian writers' schools and conferences. I began to publish articles, short stories, plays, and eventually the book *Another Day, Another Miracle* (Tyndale House, 1975).

The social activities of my former life gave way to adventures only God could have made possible. As though my life weren't already turned upside down, I began to have requests to speak to churches, Christian Women's Clubs, and seminars. This doesn't make sense. Both my husband and son are talented public speakers. Being Master of Ceremonies at banquets is fun for them, a nightmare for me.

But God knew all this. Our *infirmities* are God's *opportunities*. Had I been eloquent, I would have had no need to hang on to God. Because of my fear and helplessness, I had to prepare thoroughly and call on God constantly for help. I believe God loves a dangling Christian, totally dependent on him. That is a true cross position—dead to self, alive to Christ.

But once I step back on firm ground, I have a tendency to let my ego take over. Praise and handshaking give me a sort of "Not bad, Ceil" attitude. Of course, just at this point the glow fades until I remember the source of light and say, "Thanks once more, Lord, for loving me and holding me up. Look at the glory you stirred up."

Following that Palm Sunday, with our new adventures, scarcely without realizing it our cocktail hour was replaced with coffee time after church. It was a sort of continuous smorgasbord, delicious but fattening. We began to grow both in the Lord and around the middle.

With this new peace in our lives, the see-saw of our

individual wills was displaced by a common desire to go God's way. I was cleaning a cabinet over the refrigerator when I was surprised to find a collection of long-stemmed glasses and liqueur bottles. It was like looking at an outdated graduation dress. I could smile and say, "Was that ever a part of our lives?" With our new life all my hurt and fear of alcohol had simply been wiped away, and Hugh's thirst had evaporated as new ways satisfied him. God knew this had been a course of conflict for us, so he removed it.

Palm Sunday and the acceptance of Christ as Lord and Savior of our lives was a turning point for all three of us. My life and hands were full now. My plastic bouquet was now real. Life was fragrant, abundant, and busy.

Certainly we would face new problems, but with new power from God anything is possible.

TEN
WITHERING GRASS

It is not the will of God to give us more troubles than will bring us to live by faith in him. William Romaine

The transformation for Hugh, Senior, was radical. Business verbalizes success in dollar signs and power structure, while Jesus says, "Lay not up for yourselves treasures upon earth" (Matthew 6:19). Hugh was caught somewhere in the middle. He felt the strain of revising his goals.

First Peter 1:24, 25 began to haunt him: "For all flesh is as grass, and all the glory of man as the flower of grass. The grass withereth, and the flower thereof falleth away: but the word of the Lord endureth for ever."

Sometimes it seems God uses a spiritual sickle to prune away our pride and prestige. Old ways needed to be removed from Hugh's life, as they do from all our lives at one time or another.

At the cocktail hour of Hugh's annual Rotary Club Men's Night held at the St. Paul Athletic Club, Hugh found himself lingering in the gym. For a gregarious guy, it was ironic for him to be alone doing routine exercises while the others gathered at the bar. Later he discovered fellow nondrinkers, as well as those who didn't mind his nursing ginger ale while they downed scotch and soda. This was all part of adjusting to a new life.

However, there was no avoiding the accepted practice of

the open bar at company sponsored gatherings for invited customers. It was Hugh's job to host such affairs. He found himself feeling a new responsibility for his salesmen under such pressures.

Some five years later Hugh, together with his sales force, exhibited equipment in Hudson, Wisconsin, at a meeting of government officials. Some were users of his equipment, some nonusers. In a smoke-filled lounge and bar, Hugh sat across from an important customer, discussing future business. From the corner of his eye he saw Bill Groves, his youngest salesman, leave the bar, move toward him.

"Hugh, I have to talk to you." Bill's words were thick, eyes bloodshot. "It's very important."

"Later, Bill. Pardon this interruption, Mr. Evans. You were asking about our service policy?"

"I'm sorry, but I have to speak to you right now, Hugh." Bill's voice pled, ice rattling in the glass he held at a slant.

"You can see we're busy, Bill." Hugh's voice betrayed slight irritation. "Come back in half an hour."

"Look, Hugh." Mr. Evans stood up. "I was about to go in for dinner anyway. Why don't I meet you back here at 9:30?"

"Thanks for your understanding. This isn't at all like Bill. I'll see you here then."

Back in Bill's hotel room, Hugh scowled at his salesman, who shuffled from one foot to the other. "Bill, you know better than to interrupt a business conference like that. What's the matter with you? Looks like you need black coffee more than anything."

"I need more than that," Bill groaned. "I feel terrible. What you may not realize is that I've had a problem for a long time, been going to Alcoholics Anonymous . . . thought I had it licked . . . been on the wagon thirty days, until tonight."

Hugh stared. He hadn't realized. Sure Bill drank a little too much, but an alcoholic? "No, Bill, I didn't know your problem was that serious."

"I don't know what to do. Seems like I can't do it on my

own. I know you've found an answer, Hugh. I need your
help."
Never before had Hugh seen such despair in Bill's
normally fun-loving eyes. He noted Bill's hands, knotted
with desperation. "Please, God, give me the words for Bill.
You know how new I am at all this," Hugh prayed silently.
"You've got to turn yourself over to God, Bill. That's the
only answer I know. Are you willing to repeat a prayer with
me?"
"OK."
Both sank to their knees beside Bill's bed. Hugh led Bill
through the steps of asking forgiveness, accepting Christ,
and asking God to cure him of his problem drinking.
Bill's halting words were no longer slurred, though
interrupted at times by sniffles. Tears rolled down his
cheeks. Hugh felt tears well up in his own eyes, wiped his
cheek.
"Thanks, Hugh." Bill took a deep breath, broke out in
his familiar smile. "Somehow I think I'll make it now. Sure
sorry I broke up your conference."
"This was more important. I'll be praying for you, fellow."
A handshake and it was all over. As they headed for the
coffee shop, Hugh wondered whether Bill was sober
enough to know what he was doing.
The next morning Bill looked rested. "Hi, Hugh." Bill
squeezed Hugh's hand till it hurt. "Bet you're wondering
about last night. Yes, Hugh, I knew what I was doing and
I'm glad I did it."
That was a turning point for Bill. He took Hugh's later
suggestion to get out of the office equipment business with
its heavy drinking influence and moved into a family
restaurant business. Today he is owner and manager, with
four Christian partners, of eight restaurants, complemented
by meat and bakery subsidiaries.
For Hugh, it was a thrill to be used to help a likable young
man overcome his drinking problem—and more important,
find Christ.
But things didn't always work out so easily. After some

thirty-eight years in the same office equipment company, Hugh heard rumblings of change. With sales down because of competition from the computer industry, territories were being consolidated after years of forced expansion. Personnel cuts were frightening.

Finally the full force of change hit all four of the Twin City divisions of the company. All were to be merged into one branch location. Hugh, head of one St. Paul division, and the other three managers, totaling some 110 years of company service, were called for a conference in the Cleveland home office. None knew whether they were to be kept, reassigned, or forced to retire early. Hugh wasn't in any way prepared to retire, not with a son just starting college.

On a March day as dismal as their feelings, the four branch managers arrived in the Cleveland office. Hugh held a *Time* magazine in his hands, but later couldn't remember a word he had read. No one said much as they waited out their doom. Two were called in. Hugh glanced toward the man beside him. Both shook their heads. Waiting is a tough game with your future at stake in a world that favors youth. Hugh's turn finally came. He assumed a cheerful expression though his steps dragged.

His boss looked grim. Hugh hoped he wouldn't notice his moist hands as they shook. The usual friendly smile was absent as the talk began.

"Hugh, you can sit over there."

Hugh balanced on the edge of the armchair.

"There's no sense beating around the bush. To stay alive in today's markets, we have to compete. With competition comes change. We don't plan to keep any of you managers in the Twin Cities area."

Hugh swallowed, his lips a rigid line.

"You have a choice, Hugh," the cold voice continued. "You can either retire early, take a salesman's job in certain designated branches, or in some cases be reassigned a smaller branch."

So this is my reward for thirty-eight years of long hours, constant pressure, eight moves, Hugh thought. *These are supposed to be the golden years.*

"Think it over. Return tomorrow morning at 9:00 with your decision."

Hugh walked out of the thick carpeted office in a daze. He tried to smile at the other manager. But the smile did little to bolster the nervous man.

"Bad, eh?"

"Maybe you'll have it better." Hugh shrugged.

The men scattered, each in his own state of shock. Hugh ordered a light supper, but found even scallops stuck in his throat, dropped into a greasy wad that lay uneasily in his stomach. Coffee didn't seem to help wash it all down. In no mood to talk, Hugh went to his room with his thoughts. He retired early, but sleep was fitful. For long intervals he read Scripture, prayed, and wondered how he'd tell his family they had to move still once more, and probably to some outpost at that.

What had he done to wind up this way? All the high promise of those early years was a light now snuffed out.

Morning dragged in. The four branch managers sprawled around a table at the coffee shop. Hugh toyed with a slice of toast. It took a lot to destroy his appetite.

"Today we make our decisions."

"Some choice." The speaker stirred his coffee around and around aimlessly until it slopped into the saucer.

"Last night I was looking at Scripture recommended for situations when you're discouraged, when you feel alone, when you suffer business reverses," Hugh began. "Well, I felt they all applied to me last night. Here's what I found—do you fellows mind if I share them with you?"

Hugh began reading Psalms 23, 27, and 37. They listened politely. No comment followed.

"Time to get going." As they straggled out, Hugh thought they looked more like men going to a hanging than to a business conference. And why not? It's not easy for men in their fifties or sixties to accept possible job loss when families are in their most costly years.

The outcome was even worse than Hugh expected. "If you don't opt for retirement or a sales territory, Hugh, all we can offer you is Fargo, North Dakota."

That's impossible. Not Fargo, Hugh thought. *It's smaller than any branch even in my beginning years and the climate's bitter cold in winter, scorching in summer.* He remembered Ceil's praying for people in Fargo when it was the coldest spot in the nation. *Not that outpost!* He became aware of silence and his need to answer.

"Don't you have something in the East or South?"

"No, that's it. But, Hugh, it's not so bad. It's a growing community and not far to move."

"I can't believe that's the only opening. Ceil will hate it."

"Why not retire? You've put in a lot of years."

"With a son in college? No, that isn't possible."

It was all over in five minutes, with Hugh the new Fargo branch manager. Funny how a whole career can be junked in five minutes.

On the taxi ride to the airport, Hugh learned the fate of the others: one chose retirement, one a sales slot in San Francisco, the other a small branch in the East.

But nothing keeps Hugh down long. He has a natural resilience and optimism. Besides, now he has God. Facing my shock at the Fargo news would be the worst part of it.

"Couldn't we keep our home here in St. Paul and just rent something there?" I asked.

"That's risky with the cut in pay I'll be getting," Hugh answered.

"I thought surely this would be our last move after living in eight states already." The wistfulness in my voice cut through Hugh. "Somehow we always seem to get farther away from New England."

"I know, honey, but I had no choice."

God was close that day, and all the days ahead. He listened as Hugh and I prayed, talked, and sought verses in the Bible for needed guidance. God is a present help in trouble. He really is.

Plans were soon made and a travel trailer purchased,

Hugh's Fargo home during the several months it took to sell our St. Paul house. A small townhouse across the river in Moorehead, Minnesota, became our new home, stuffed with bulky antique furniture.

Hugh set off to work with survival equipment stored in his car trunk and long underwear under his business suit. That's a way of life in the icy hamlets he visited. By year's end, Hugh had logged many miles. But with God's help he secured one of the largest orders of his career, from a leading snowmobile manufacturer. This, together with other good orders from his inspired sales force, placed him in line for the President's Award, a sterling silver trophy. To everyone's astonishment, at the annual Hundred Club celebration Hugh received the Davis Cup for having attained the highest percentage of quota of any branch in the United States over a six-month contest period.

Hugh enjoyed these honors after his rough treatment the year before.

Such glory was short-lived. Out came the sickle. This time Hugh was told the bad news by telephone. After two years in Fargo, further consolidations and territorial reorganizations caused the company to close the Fargo branch. This time he was given no choice but early retirement at sixty-two. Hugh studied real estate, hoping to recoup that way.

But God had other plans. On our return move to the Twin Cities and the purchase of what seemed like a dollhouse, Hugh received a call from president Carl Lundquist of Bethel College in St. Paul.

"Hugh, welcome back to the Twin Cities. There's something I'd like to discuss with you. Can you meet me at my office this afternoon?"

It has now been five years since Hugh accepted the position of assistant to the president of Bethel College for the salary of $1.00 a year. They have been good years, learning how the academic world runs, getting to know faculty and students in God-centered relationships.

"For richer or poorer." That's what Hugh pledged in

marriage. That works in a career too. At a dollar a year, inflation can be rough. But less is more—this is what Hugh has come to discover as God enables him to see much of the country, representing Bethel. As God gives him time to build copies of antique furniture. As God blesses his children and grandchildren. Yes, everything does work together for good for those who love the Lord . . . ultimately.

Sometimes weeds need to be pulled out of our lives. That's when God gets out the sickle and cuts away at the old Hugh (or Ceil).

All flesh is as grass, but God's Word does go on forever.

But difficult as we found our business situation, others were experiencing far greater trouble, as we learned from a letter from Jim and Eleanor Fox in Cleveland.

ELEVEN
SCRUBBING WITH GOD
Empathy is your pain in my heart. Halford E. Luccock

It was a gloomy January morning. Jim and Eleanor sat by
their daughter Shelley's hospital bed in Cleveland, Ohio.
They were utterly exhausted. It had been 111 days since
they first brought Shelley, twenty one, into the hospital for
what seemed a minor illness. Since then, her condition had
daily worsened. She now lay unconscious. With each
passing day she sank closer to death.

Many parents would have broken long before this point.
But God had been their daily companion ever since the
birth of their first daughter, Holly, whom they discovered to
be retarded. Instead of folding under that blow, Jim began
giving festive dinners to groups with a variety of needs, with
help from his Wesley Class members at Cleveland's Church
of the Savior. (I have described this more fully in my earlier
book.)

Trouble also hit their third child, Charles III. A series of
problems with his leg finally were resolved with the
amputation of the leg in 1974. But with faith, much support
from loving friends, plus an encouraging letter from
Senator Ted Kennedy, they weathered those traumatic
days.

Shelley, their second child, came into the family with a

bright mind and love for all around her. What a comfort she was to her parents, a special dividend through all the difficult needs of their other children.

But she too suffered problems. While in sixth grade, it was discovered that the duct that controlled the water pressure in her brain cavity was blocked. Miraculously she had suffered no brain damage. A shunt was installed successfully. Later surgery was again required to replace shunts to keep the blocked duct open.

However, in October of 1975 infection reappeared around the last shunt, causing severe injury to the brain. Her doctor, a renowned neurosurgeon, had seen Shelley through earlier illness, and under the charm of her bright spirit had come to love her as a daughter.

During the days that followed, one crisis came after another for Shelley. During these times, when questioned by Shelley's parents, "What are you going to do now?" the doctor often replied, "I'm going to pray a lot." The hospital corridors were carpeted with prayer those days by doctors, nurses, parents, and friends throughout the city.

Her doctor felt it was important to keep Shelley awake. A guest register was placed by her bed along with a sign, "Wake Shelley up." Jim says, "I really couldn't count the number of people who sat by her bed when we weren't with her. Some visited almost every day for four months. I hardly worked for those four months. When I did, my boss said, 'What are you doing here? You belong with Shelley.'"

On Friday, January 8, Eleanor and Jim watched their doctor's face as he examined Shelley. It was agony to sit by, helpless. There was no response on Shelley's once bright face. Her fingers lay rigid, her figure a stiff mound on the bed though once she ran toward life smiling.

The examination took longer than usual. Finally the doctor raised his head, stared a moment out the window. Jim and Eleanor waited silently, unmoving. Their minds refused to think.

Slowly the doctor shook his head. "It's as I feared," he said. "She's terminal. Unless we can reverse whatever is going on in her brain in forty-eight to seventy-two hours, we're going to lose her." His voice broke as he looked sadly into Jim and Eleanor's eyes, his own filled with tears.

He clasped and unclasped his slender fingers. Suddenly he stood up. "I can't give up now. There's just one chance in a hundred we can save her, but I have to take it, make one more try . . . I'd like to operate at 10:30."

Stunned, Jim drew in a long breath, shifted his feet. "Maybe I should take you off the case, put the 'Man upstairs' in charge." A half-smile softened his tense mouth. After all, God had always been in charge.

The doctor caught the glimmer of hope in Jim's voice. "A wise choice. May I scrub with the Great Physician?"

At 10:30 that Sunday morning Shelley once more was rushed into surgery. This operation revealed heretofore undiscovered pressure in the third ventricle of the brain, pressure which was choking her brain.

Seven A.M. Monday found the tired group of parents, brother, friends, and surgeon watching the girl who had now lain in a deep coma for four days.

Eleanor and Jim watched the doctor fold his stethoscope, study the sleeping girl. "She seems fractionally improved," he said. They exchanged glances. Eleanor's lips moved in prayer. They settled back to watch once more.

At 9:30 Shelley's hand moved, her eyes fluttered open, moved from one person to another. "Hi," she whispered, then fell back into a healthy sleep.

Word spread quickly down the hall. Instead of deep gloom, the hospital floor now radiated joy. Phones buzzed the good news to hundreds praying around the city.

Prayer continued as Shelley improved. Recuperation was to take years, sometimes slowed with minor reverses. But it was certain that Shelley would recover. Praise God!

Jim's letter to us said in part, "Your letter, like a comforting hand out of the past, brought a great deal of joy and solace at a very trying time. I had repeated the Twenty-Third Psalm many times in my life by rote, but we have now walked through the valley of the shadow of death.

Our faith and our friends represented 'his rod and his staff.'
Now surely with Shelley back home with us 'the table is set
before us.' People we never knew, from all over the city,
called and asked if they might pray for Shelley. It was prayer
that brought her home."

Eleanor and Jim have been a "lamp" to many with their
enduring faith, and in turn God has answered their prayers
as Jesus promised—"I will not leave you comfortless" (John
14:18). God comforts us, and in turn, we can comfort
others (see 2 Corinthians 1:4).

I went back to Jim's words, "Your letter, like a comforting
hand . . ." Not only did I want to shout with joy at Shelley's
miraculous healing, but I marveled that a little act like
sending a note and a copy of my book had comforted others
in their suffering. It is good to be used of God. It is good to
be alert to the needs of others. God's timing is best.

Time after time God has pressed me to send a copy of my
book to someone, often without knowing their special
need. Just a week earlier I had received a letter from a
college friend in Cleveland to whom I previously felt called
to send a book. She answered, "We'd put off returning
home to Cleveland from Florida. Somehow the thought of
returning home after Mother's death without her there to
greet us was more than I wanted to face. When we finally
did return, there was a stack of mail on the hall table. On
top was your book. I sat right down and started to read.
When I read the chapter about your mother's death, tears
streamed down my cheeks, but somehow it comforted me.
Thank you for helping me over a hard time."

Helping each other over a difficult time—isn't that what
the Christian life is all about? I opened Jim's letter once
more to reread a postscript:

"One day during Shelley's illness, we came into her
hospital room to find tears coursing down her face.

" 'Why tears, dear, just when things are getting better?'

" 'I'm crying because I'm so happy—happy because we
have so many friends.'

" 'That should make you rejoice, not cry, Shelley dear.'

" 'It does, but I'm crying for all the people who don't have such friends to support them.'"

Jim admits there were days when he felt like yelling, "God, get off my back." But he was able to endure adversity by living one day at a time with God, while bolstered by loving friends.

It may well be that we can't all face up to trouble as do the valiant Jims and Eleanors of this world, but each of us can scrub with God and do our part, giving comfort and finding comfort as God directs us.

TWELVE
"I AM WITH YOU"

I think of death as a glad awakening from this troubled sleep which we call life; as an emancipation from a world which, beautiful though it be, is still a land of captivity. Lyman Abbott

"I am with you always, even to the end of the world."

Marilyn Bohne had often heard these words of Christ, but her world seemed to stretch gloriously ahead of her that snowy December evening in St. Paul, Minnesota. She had no hint then of the tragedy to follow; but God, with his infinite love, was preparing her for future hurt.

Marilyn sniffed the crisp air as her husband, Quentin, edged into a parking place three blocks from the auditorium where Bethel College's Festival of Music was about to begin. Their footsteps crunched on the snowy sidewalk as they walked arm in arm. Marilyn smiled up at him, a question in her eyes. Did he possibly remember?

"Do you know, sweetheart," Marilyn mused, "this is the very street we walked on our first date . . . Can it be seventeen years ago? And we became engaged at the Christmas Festival a few months after that." Marilyn's eyes crinkled. "This is our engagement anniversary. So much has happened since then."

"I love you even more now." Quentin squeezed her hand.

"Me too." The eagerness on her husband's face was so like the young man who had hinted at his love long ago at this very spot! Marilyn's heart overflowed with joy. How

could she say all that lay in her heart—the blessings of four
healthy children, a lake home designed by Quentin, plus
years of sharing God's love with Bethel students. "Tonight
is really an anniversary of our love," she said.
The festive mood continued into breakfast the next
morning. Quentin glanced far out over their frozen lake.
"It's a perfect day for skating."
Marilyn followed his glance. Not a bad day for horseback
riding either, she thought wistfully as she added up the day's
chores.
As though sensing her mood, Quentin offered to help
with the routine cleaning, then settled down to a weekly
football game from which ordinarily nothing distracted him.
At halftime, to Marilyn's astonishment, he turned off the
game.
"Come on. Let's saddle up the horses." Marilyn slipped
on riding boots quickly before he could change his mind.
They cantered along the lake's edge to a lonely peninsula.
Both blinked at sun reflecting snow crystals on pine
branches. Marilyn scooped a frozen clump, examined
myriad patterns. "How lovely."
"God's in each snowflake, just as in every detail of our
lives," Quentin marveled. Their glance lingered on the quiet
lake. Finally Marilyn sighed, turned her horse toward home.
Such moments as these were rare, thanks to their different
teaching schedules and the children's activities.
It was after four when Marilyn swung out of the drive
with their three sons, off for groceries. She caught a glimpse
of Quentin's jacket as he skated over the ice, enjoying the
pleasure he had delayed in order to go horseback riding
with his wife. Lauri, their thirteen-year-old daughter, and
her friend, Carol, skated close behind. Their wool caps
bounced like bright dots.
When Marilyn and her sons returned from shopping, it
was pitch dark. Even before she saw their house blazing
with lights, Marilyn sensed something was terribly wrong.
Cars sprawled at odd angles, a police car sat close to the
garage. Her heart lurched.

Scarcely knowing what she did, she grabbed two heavy bags of groceries, and stepped out on the icy walk as the boys ran through the basement entry. Never had she felt so cold, so alone. "Oh, Lord," she breathed.

It was then she felt a softness around her, a gentle touch at her elbow, a quiet voice beside her—"You don't know what you are going into, but remember *I am with you.*" Eerie shadows turned friendly. God's presence was all around . . . and with it strength and security.

The door opened, splashed light at her feet. Someone took her groceries, led her upstairs. Lauri, wrapped in a blanket, reached out for her, then buried her face on her mother's shoulder.

"Where . . . " She scanned the room. "Quent? No, oh, no," she cried out.

Hands eased her to the sofa. Lauri sat next to her.

"Please tell me what's happened."

"Oh, Mother." Lauri's sobs were the only sound in the room as the others waited in awkward silence.

"Please."

"Carol and I were skating backwards," Lauri began, "and you know how careful Daddy always is. He told us that was OK at rinks, but not on lakes, so we turned around. I circled. Daddy and Carol skated out. Then I heard Carol gasp. There was a crunching sound. I couldn't see them." She closed her eyes, grimaced. "When I got there, all I could see was a dark hole in the ice. Then Daddy came up. I reached for him, but he yelled, 'Help Carol first.'"

"He would. Go on."

"I grabbed for her arm, but she was too far away. So I lay flat on the ice. That way I could reach farther. This time I got a real hold, but the ice broke off as I pulled. She flattened out, and I was able to ease her up onto solid ice."

"Oh, honey, thank God."

"She left for help. I moved over toward Daddy. It was hard to see, bitter cold. His sleeve was icy. It slipped from my fingers. He drifted out. He seemed numb . . . almost unconscious. When I tried to reach him, the ice kept breaking off. Finally, I grabbed his wrist and pulled with all my strength. The next thing I knew, I had broken through and Daddy had disappeared." Lauri's voice broke. She bit her lip.

"I dived under, but all I could see was blackness. I tried and tried until I could hardly move." Lauri shivered with the memory.

"Oh, darling . . . How did you get out?"

"I don't know; God must have helped me. I found myself sitting on the ice. I didn't know what to do, Mother. I wanted to jump back in. I stayed there a long, long time and it got so dark. Finally, I just . . . just started walking to the farm where Carol had gone for help."

"It's a good thing she didn't go back into the water, Mrs. Bohne," an officer spoke up. "Our diver went down. There's a deep spring there that accounts for the soft spot in the ice. We'll have to wait until morning to send our divers back. I'm sorry, ma'am."

Marilyn's hand covered her mouth. "Quentin, Quentin."

"If only I could have saved Dad!"

Marilyn hugged Lauri to her. "God has an appointed time for each of us," she said.

That night with the house quiet and Lauri finally asleep beside her, Marilyn lay wide awake. Strangely, in spite of that cold lake just outside her window she felt warm and protected. The terrible truth was there and the horror, but it was as though God had tucked her in. She knew many were praying. It was like a shield around her. She couldn't pray at such a time, but still God seemed so close, so able to hold and help her.

Past events paraded before her—that walk with Quentin, his comment about the snowflake, cleaning house together for company they had no idea would come. Like a revelation, the truth hit. God had been preparing her for this moment. She saw Quentin's love for her twisting and turning all the way to heaven like a strand of silver. *I'm not alone now and I never will be*, she thought as she turned over and dropped into sleep.

Many wondered how Marilyn kept her radiant smile through the funeral and rough days of starting life anew. "God prepared me for my loss," she told them. "As we walked that last walk together and later rode over the snow, we were one in love and one in Christ. Quentin lives with the Lord now, but our love goes on and God has promised that he will give me the strength and the power I need in the days ahead."

He has, though it took much prayer, prayer to help Lauri and Carol find peace with their survival despite Quentin's death, prayer to help Marilyn in her struggle to achieve her master's degree in teaching while ministering to her family's growing needs, prayer to help her as counselor to lonely international students in this country. Yes, God prepared her, so this gentle woman could be a rock for others.

Many times I have experienced God's help when trouble hits, but until I heard Marilyn's story I hadn't realized that God personally prepared us for our trials. But of course preparation is a heavenly principle—whether it is John the Baptist saying, "Prepare to meet your Messiah," Jesus trying to prepare his disciples for his coming death on the cross, or Jesus saying, "I go to prepare a place for you. In my Father's house are many mansions" (John 14:2).

None of us wants bad times, but it is how we accept them that counts the most. I've found that putting the facts together with unknowns before God is the first step toward facing a storm, much as we batten down the shutters on a beach house before a hurricane. God is a sufficient refuge before and during any trouble he allows to come our way.

THIRTEEN
HEALER OF THE SOUL
Life doesn't begin at forty, or at twenty, but at Calvary.
Elaine Kilgore

A few months after Marilyn Bohne told me of her husband's home-going, I learned that my younger brother Bill, in New Jersey, was ill with emphysema. It wasn't long before I received sad news from Bill's wife, Karen: "Your brother Bill is worse, back in the hospital. The doctors call his condition terminal, with weeks, months, or perhaps a year to live. All they can do is ease his suffering."

Terminal. I couldn't believe that ugly word. He was only fifty-five. Bill, the kid brother who played father to my dolls; Bill, the returned soldier with big dreams and a bad case of malaria; Bill, who always welcomed us with a broad grin. He would soon leave this earth, unless a miracle happened. We prayed that God would restore Bill. But meanwhile there was so much I longed to talk about with him, things we never mentioned on quick pop-through visits.

Did he really know God? He was head deacon in his church, but after reading *Another Day, Another Miracle*, he'd written, "Being active in church doesn't necessarily mean you're close to God."

Time was running out for Bill. I felt caged in by terrible

questions. Would it tire Bill too much if I visited him? Would it add to his wife's already hectic schedule as night clerk at a nearby hospital? I decided after much prayer and an invitation from Karen to go for a brief visit.

On the plane I prayed, "O God, let there be healing for Bill, also for my sister with a marriage problem, and for my older brother losing his home by mortgage foreclosure—but most of all healing in the total family relationship to you." Our problems sounded like a soap opera, but sometimes that's the way it is.

Bill was thin as a skeleton, his eyes enormous with a new sadness. He dragged his feet because of muscles destroyed by cortisone. Sometimes he could talk; at other times he struggled for each breath. Long hours he sat using a nebulizer machine, which helped break up mucus in lungs no longer able to do the job.

My preparing a sandwich for Bill's lunch helped save his breath so that he was able to eat it. The slightest effort weakened him. I had prayed to be able to help. I was glad I could fit into the family pattern.

But God's kingdom here on earth and in heaven—that was what really mattered. Could God use me? I felt more like a clumsy maid than a ministering angel.

But at the same time I sensed an undercurrent of God's love working among us. Even though I rose in the morning just before Karen tumbled wearily into bed after night hospital duty, there was a rhythm to our living together, even with Scott, twenty-one, and Brad, fifteen, leaving for work and school respectively at different hours.

My first evening there, after seeing Karen off for work I sat by Bill's hospital bed that now crowded their dining room. "It's terrible to be so useless," he began. "Up until recently I've at least been able to help with shopping." He stopped to catch his breath, lay back to rest. Bill felt left out, used up; and for someone who had been a civic leader and head deacon in his church, this wasn't easy to take.

"I feel guilty now because I brought all this trouble on

my family just when I should be looking after them. How many times Karen begged me to stop smoking . . . and I just kept on."

"We all do things we wish we hadn't, Bill. Maybe you can help someone else stop smoking before it's too late for them."

He shook his head sadly. "If I could just get well, but the doctors—well, you know. . . ."

"Yes, but Bill, if God has a plan to use you, he can heal you just like that." His hand smoothed the bed while he stared into space.

"Besides, Bill, you've done something at which many men fail. You've raised four sons to be outstanding young men—not selfish mixed-up kids, but boys who love you and care about others. That's no small gift these days."

"Being a father is important."

"You bet it is. After all, there's nothing more important to God than being a Father to us. How he must rejoice over each successful father on earth."

As our conversation continued, I noticed dry skin scaling on Bill's swollen ankles. I rubbed lotion over the swelling, felt the boniness of his legs, once strong and muscular. I blinked back tears.

"Look here, I can't wear you out my first night or Karen will send me home."

For hours I lay in bed hearing the clock chime, picturing Bill's smile and his wasted body.

Bill felt well enough to sit in the living room with us a bit the next evening. Karen's blue hospital smock was a good contrast with her enormous brown eyes. "How's your mother doing, Karen? It's about a year since your father's death, isn't it?

Karen's eyes clouded, her hands twisted. "Yes, almost. Mom's . . . Well, it's not good. She misses Dad terribly. We both do." Her voice broke. "Mother speaks often about the words of the young minister at Dad's funeral. She wishes she could believe in heaven and seeing Dad again. I do too."

She leaned forward, her eyes dark with hurt. "You know our old neighbor, Bernice Carlson?"

"Yes."

"She's so sure about heaven."

Bill broke in. "We went to her husband Bert's funeral. It was really something."

"When I saw Bernice, I put my arms around her, but I was crying so hard I couldn't say a word. You know what she said? She said, 'Don't cry for Bert. He's at home with God. He's alive and well. What could be more wonderful than that? Instead of tears, rejoice for him.'"

"And what's more, she meant it," Bill added. Karen nodded.

I smiled at their eagerness. "I don't doubt it, knowing them. Bert's been part of God's family a long time. That's what God wants for all of us. He sacrificed his Son, Jesus, on the cross so that you and I and Bert might have eternal life, might be freed from our selfishness that turns us away from God. All we need to do is receive Jesus in order to become God's children and inherit life in his heavenly kingdom."

"If only I could know." Karen shook her head slowly.

"But Karen, you can. God's promise is as real as this table." I thumped the table before me. "My mother and Grandmother Riggs lived by God's Word and promises. I know they are in heaven today, alive with God. Bill, you remember how Grandmother depended on God. Don't you feel sure they are in heaven with God?"

He thought a minute. "Yes, I'm positive of it."

But Karen had had enough for one evening. She stood up, shrugged with a little laugh. "Well, there are some things I must do for myself. I don't expect God to unload the dishwasher."

A little later Karen, about to leave for work, hugged me at the door. "For someone not very religious, I sure talk to God a lot these days on my way to work. Often it's just, 'Lord, get me through today.'"

Monday evening was Bill's and Karen's 29th wedding anniversary. Bill phoned a delicatessen friend to send cold cuts and salad so Karen wouldn't have to cook, then ordered a bouquet of her favorite yellow roses. Their oldest son, Billy, and his wife joined Scott, Brad, and myself for a celebration evening. Bill's eyes were soft with love for Karen as she opened their gifts: a stained glass plant holder designed by Billy, checks from the kids' earnings, a phone for Bill by his bed, hand controls for his TV, and other thoughtful gifts.

Silently I thanked God for letting me be there, to feel the flow of their love. I asked God to bring us all to him in his own time and way.

My last day with Bill was a quiet one, for which I was glad. I fixed him a soft-boiled egg and sipped coffee while he used a nebulizer. I dreaded leaving him. He sensed my concern, told me how much my visit and our quiet chats had meant to him.

Then he turned off the machine. His green eyes studied me.

"I've learned something," he began. "When your Gail told us how you and Hugh had gone off the 'deep end,' as she put it, and had become superreligious, you had Steve and me worried. We figured if it affected your own daughter that way, we better watch out."

He paused. "But I think I understand her attitude now. She loved you and Hugh as she knew you and didn't want you changed into something different, especially if that new you left her out. I suspect she's hanging on to the past until she feels comfortable in the present."

I was amazed at how he had grasped the crux of the matter and flinched that Gail's words might have alienated my brothers. "You're probably right, Bill."

"But as for me . . . " He stopped, took a breath. "I see now that you and Hugh are really born again." I was surprised that he knew the phrase used by Jesus in John 3:3, meaning that a spiritual rebirth has taken place through acceptance of Jesus as Lord and Savior. "You're so filled with love and joy, and your whole attitude toward material things has changed. God has changed you and it's great."

The nebulizer went on and off. "Now, don't get me wrong. I'm not born again, but I'm glad it's happened to you."

Steve came then to drive me to the airport. It was doubly hard to leave with Bill's words echoing in my head, "I'm not born again." I kept thinking about Jesus' words, "Except a man be born again, he cannot see the kingdom of God."

Lord, more than anything I want the kingdom of heaven for my brother—yes, more than the healing of his body, as much as I want that.

June arrived and with it another brief visit to Bill, now completely bedfast at home, needing more nursing care than was available. Hugh sponge-bathed him, and together we cared for him while Karen was at work.

Even though Bill was much worse physically, in another way he was better, more at peace, eager for prayer. Bill slept as I knitted close by, while Hugh mowed the lawn.

"Ceil . . ." Bill's voice startled me. "Thanks so much for *The Hiding Place* you gave me. Just finished reading it."

"That's odd. I had forgotten sending the book, Bill."

"You sent it last year, but I just finished reading it. It meant so much to me."

"I'm glad. I loved it too." His eyes were already closing again. I thought about the scene in which Corrie's sister lay dying. Her beautiful faith must have touched Bill. That prison camp was horrible, but Bill was a prisoner of his illness. Maybe it was this book that had made the change in Bill.

Too soon it was time to leave for a conference in Hartford. God willing, we would see Bill on our return in two weeks.

By then Bill lay in critical condition at Montclair Hospital. Tubes dripped fluid into his veins, a nurse administered oxygen. He seemed too weak to shift his cramped legs. The whites of his eyes were a sickly yellow, but he knew us. As the nurse moved to the adjoining patient, Bill slid his oxygen mask aside and gazed at us.

"Did you have a good time?"

I couldn't answer. How do you tell a brother in such agony the joy of romping in ocean waves and warm sunshine? "It was beautiful," was all I could manage. If I could only carry him out where he could float free in cool water!

"I'm glad." He understood.

"Can you sleep at night, Bill?"

"Yes, sleep is good, but it's terrible to wake up."

I stroked his cold hand. The nurse came over. "It's time to go."

I leaned over to kiss him. My tears wet his cheek.

"I'll love you forever, Bill dear."

He nodded. His pain-filled eyes followed us all the way out. We both knew it was good-bye until we would meet in heaven. *Oh, God, how it hurts to say good-bye here on earth. Bill has to be yours. I believe he is.*

Two days later Karen called us in Pennsylvania. "Bill passed away an hour ago," she said. We discussed funeral arrangements. "But there is something I must tell you," she continued. "Two days after you left for Hartford, I found Bill in a coma. When he regained consciousness in the hospital, we asked him if he remembered our talking to him then. 'No,' he said, 'but there is something I do remember. I was floating through beautiful clouds toward heaven. And I could breathe again. I could breathe deeply.'" Karen's voice trembled over the phone. "Wasn't that strange, Ceil?"

"Yes, strange and wonderful," I answered. "I believe it was God's way of reassuring all of us that Bill now belongs to God."

We marveled at how God cared for Bill's earthly needs, but even more for his spiritual needs, taking him each step of the way. I have no idea why God didn't heal his body, but God has shown me that though he often does heal us and rejoices in doing so, spiritual healing takes precedence. And at the same time, he cares about the whole family. Back when I was an active doer, God laid me aside for months with a painful back. Without this thoughtful time, I would probably never have become a seeker, nor a finder, nor indeed a writer. God has his own reasons, beyond our knowledge. Bill at fifty-six seemed too young to go, but I am confident his death will not be in vain and I am thankful that he met God in time.

Jesus established these priorities long ago when the woman with a chronic hemorrhage touched his robe. "Daughter, thy faith hath made thee whole," Jesus said (Mark 5:34) and she was healed in mind and body. Bill is now whole, and we all grew through his suffering.

FOURTEEN
EMPTY CHAIRS

*It is so much easier to tell a person what to do with his problem
than to stand with him in his pain.* David Augsburger

On a July visit back to Wyomissing, Pennsylvania, we found
our former neighborhood even lovelier than we
remembered it. The fragrance of roses and honeysuckle
drifted in through the open window. The smell of frying
bacon lured us to the kitchen where our hostess, Peg, a
widow of several years, lined crisp strips of bacon on a
platter. Peg's kitchen gleamed. Geraniums nodded a
welcome.

"I hope you slept well," Peg said.

Peg's warm voice and friendly smile must be a tonic to her
hospital patients, I thought. Widowhood hadn't seemed to
dim her exuberance.

"Hugh, you sit there and Ceil over by the window."

As I bit into a frosted roll, I became aware of Peg's dark
eyes as they rested on Hugh across the table. Unaware of
her glance, he scooped bacon and egg onto his fork. Peg's
eyes met mine. Her unmasked pain shocked me. Peg's
haunting loneliness lay just under the surface.

"How is it really for you, Peg?" I asked.

"I'm grateful for my work." She toyed with her spoon.
"It's strange, some of the situations that seem the easiest,
such as holidays with the children and grandchildren, turn

out to be the hardest. I suppose that's because Al loved
them so much, and I want to share those times with him."
    "I hadn't thought of it that way."
    "My worst time was facing Al's empty chair. See, he put
the children's pictures there under the glass of our tabletop
where he could see them first thing each morning."
    We noted snapshots lined in a half-circle facing Hugh.
    "For days after Al's death, I carried trays into the den by
the TV. Finally I realized I was running away from his chair.
That day I set my place at Al's. Somehow sitting in his seat
wasn't as bad as looking at it empty. I was already looking
after household accounts, keeping the car running, hanging
my own pictures. This was another step I had to take. But it
certainly wasn't easy. It still isn't."
    As she spoke, I thought about how much we take widows
and widowers for granted. Sure, we visit the funeral home,
send in food, tell them we're sorry. But from then on, all
too often it's up to them. They can shovel their drives, eat
alone, slide into an empty pew with no one noticing. We've
done our duty.
    Perhaps even more so if we've put the widow or widower
on a high spiritual pedestal. I've made that misjudgment
more than once.
    It had been ten years since the start of Marilyn Bohne's
experiences with God in widowhood. With such faith and
control she could really make it, I felt. We had prayed for
her in difficult times—for example, when real estate
transactions went askew.
    One Sunday afternoon during Bethel Choir's Festival
weekend, twelve of us, all members of an active prayer
chain, gathered with our husbands for our annual dinner.
After hot cider, we sat down at two long tables shining with
silver and thin goblets. Marilyn was late, but no one was
surprised—she lived farthest away.
    Just as we started serving, the front door burst open. We
stared as Marilyn hurried in, followed by her youngest son,
Brent. We quickly slid over to set up an extra place for him.
With a healthy appetite, he dug in to a heaped plate.

Marilyn sipped water, buttered her roll slowly. Not sure
what was wrong, we ate in awkward silence.
"I almost didn't come," she finally stated, eyes brimming
tears. She bit her lip, but it didn't stop tears from splashing
down. "You see . . ."
"Now, Mom," her son interrupted. His hand covered
hers in a boyish gesture. She tried to smile at him, but her
chin trembled.
"Today is the anniversary of Quentin's death. I felt I
couldn't come alone here with all you couples. I was going
to stay home. But Brent persuaded me, said he'd be my
escort."
Brent looked small and a bit embarrassed at the table's
end.
"Yesterday when I was moping around," she continued,
"Brent, who doesn't care about riding, noticed. I was
startled when he asked me to go riding with him. When we
finished and he dismounted, Quint's horse nuzzled him.
Brent asked me if the horse did that to everybody who rode
him. I assured him the horse was telling him he liked being
ridden by Brent."
Brent grinned at us, shrugged his shoulders, and gave his
mother a broad smile. Reassured, he turned back to his
dinner. With Marilyn relaxed, conversation flowed freely.
Through this incident I realized the fallacy that those of
strong faith suffer less than others. It seems that love, cut
off, hurts the faithful the same as the ungodly. People-lifters
at times need lifting themselves, but they, like Marilyn who
frequently helps international students solve their
problems, may be hesitant to make their own needs known.
Being blessed with a dear husband by my side through
forty years of marriage, I am only beginning to realize how
little I understand the loneliness of those who have lost
mates through death, divorce, or separation, or of those
who never had the joy of a married partner. As I talk to the
bereft, I realize how shallow my caring for others has been.
With this awareness I have determined to tuck records of
deaths, divorces, strayed children into my birthday book so

that on the anniversaries of these tragic dates, I can plan
something to offset the hurt. Love is the greatest gift we
have to give. I pray that God will help all of us to be more
sensitive to loneliness wherever it exists.

In a recent Christmas season, Hugh and I were invited to
a candlelight supper at the home of Charlotte, a widow of
only seven months. Over past years we had often been
entertained in her home, usually with some international
students. This evening Charlotte's home sparkled as usual
with holly and candles. She confessed that when she hung
the decorations, she could hardly see through her tears.
Taking out the boxes carefully packed away by her husband,
climbing a ladder as he did to hang a wreath on the
balcony—Charlotte found this hard to do.

"I figure it's up to me now," Charlotte said, "I can be
gloomy and skip decorating, or get going." She led us
upstairs, introduced us to a student from Hong Kong and
one from Ethiopia. Yes, Charlotte was taking steps one at a
time as she began new life as a single person. But best of all,
she was continuing the ministry begun with her husband,
that of helping lonely international students find a home
relationship.

This week I talked to a new grandfather whose wife had
been in Kansas City for two weeks to help their daughter
care for the new baby. He had another lonely week to go,
over Christmas and New Year's at that. "This has been a
good experience for me," Howard said. "Now I realize how
it feels to drive alone to church, sit alone, go home alone
and fix dinner. Now that I understand this feeling, I hope
I'll do more to help lonely people."

Hugh and I agreed with him. But just how, we wondered.
Meals on wheels is one way to help lonely shut-ins. We
heard of a Twin City church that took on the ambitious
assignment of registering people's talents for an exchange:
baby-sitting for fixing drippy faucets, painting and raking for
sewing repairs. Perhaps we can initiate some such service.

I've never forgotten a report I read about London under
seige during the Nazi "blitz." At that time, a warden in each

neighborhood knew the occupants of each house, their
health needs, and other vital statistics in case of disaster.
Why should we wait for disaster? Maybe Hugh and I can
be sort of neighborhood wardens and be ready to give
whatever help is needed.

I have read that even that spiritual giant, author C. S.
Lewis, went through deep struggles at the death of his
beloved wife after just four years of marriage. At first, Lewis
railed at God in his agony.[5] But he found that ranting only
cut him off from God as well as his wife. Then after facing
up to his problem, he discovered that in praising God he
came out of the shadows, back into the light.

"Grief," says Lewis, "is like a long valley, a winding valley
where any bend may reveal a totally new landscape. I think I
am beginning to understand why grief feels like suspense. It
comes from the frustration of so many impulses that had
become habitual. Thought after thought, feeling after
feeling, action after action had H. (his wife) for their object.
Now their target is gone. I keep on through habit fitting an
arrow to the string; then I remember and have to lay the
bow down. So many roads lead thought to H. I set out on
one of them. But now there's an impassable frontier-post
across it."

As Christian neighbors, we must help the bereaved adjust
to their loss. I was glad Hugh could warm Al's empty chair
for a moment. There are many empty chairs. We can't ever
really fill them, only serve as instruments to relieve the
emptiness one step at a time.

FIFTEEN
WHEN GOD CALLS

I have been dying for twenty years. Now I am going to live.
Last words of James Burns

For some, heaven is an ethereal land lacking significance in
our workaday world. For others, heaven seems more real
and more lasting than life here. To the latter, heaven
beckons as a future homeland, while earthly life serves as
but a brief preview of our eternal life in heaven.

Throughout our lives here God speaks to us in many
ways. Sadly, many of his calls never get through. Either we
aren't listening, or we're too busy to consider what he has to
say (or too apathetic), or our sins bring spiritual static into
our souls. Whatever the reason, we lose spiritual blessing
through our communication breakdown. The key to really
knowing God is constant prayer, which actually involves
both listening to God as well as taking requests to him.

The question of homeland can be confusing to displaced
persons—all around is alien. For several years Pastor Phan
Minh Tan was minister to three Vietnamese churches in the
St. Paul, Minnesota, area. His people, accustomed to
tropical weather, found transportation problems unbearable
when their cars froze at 40° below zero. At a service held a
year after they left Vietnam, Pastor Tan preached on the
theme, "My people, you have three homelands: your
beloved one left behind, this one where you have been

kindly received, and your future homeland, heaven." He
knew that with God's help we can overcome any obstacle
and keep our vision on our eternal destiny: going home to
be with God.

My friend Bert Carlson had been looking forward to
heaven all his life. On November 22 he was in intensive
care at a hospital in Montclair, New Jersey. About 10 P.M. a
close family friend, Pat Macauley, received a call from God
to pray for Bert. She did. Sleep was slow in coming. During
the night, she wakened. The room was filled with a warm
light. Before her eyes appeared a beautiful dream or vision,
in glowing color. She saw a choir of joyful people singing
music lovelier than any she had ever heard. As the music
faded, a voice said, "It's all right, Bert, it won't be long now.
We're waiting for you."

Pat blinked. Was she awake or dreaming? The clock
showed 1:15 A.M. Only later did she tell Bert's wife,
Bernice, of her unusual experience.

The following morning, Bernice sat beside Bert's hospital
bed praying. Suddenly Bert half raised himself.

"Honey, you're stepping on my robe," he called.

Bernice glanced at his bathrobe on the foot of the bed,
turned back to him puzzled. Bert appeared to look up as if
seeing someone. His face beamed with a radiant smile.
"Oh," he said, "I have to get up." He fell back, his eyes
closed, and slipped off to glory.

Later that evening before Bernice could sleep, her
bedroom suddenly became very bright. Bernice, knowing
nothing of Pat's experience, saw a large choir of happy
people, clothed in white choir robes. To the right she saw a
man hurriedly slipping his right arm into the sleeve of his
robe. He then stepped into the front row to join the singing
choir, his face shining with happiness. "It was Bert!"
Bernice says. "I wondered if I were dreaming. So I asked,
'Lord Jesus, if this is really true, please let me see it again.'
He did. The vision was repeated."

The next day when Pat told Bernice of her vision, they
marveled over God's way of summoning his children to

heaven and at the same time communicating to those near to the loved one. It was then that Jesus' words— "Whosoever liveth and believeth in me shall never die" (John 11:26)—gained special meaning for Bernice. In the days that followed both Bert's and Bill's homecomings to heaven, I often thought back to my father's death and funeral some seven years earlier. The thought of Dad blocked from both heaven and heavenly reunions with loved ones was agony for me. Yet, search as I might, I couldn't remember any remark of his that indicated a relationship with God. He said nothing unfavorable to God, but Jesus says, "If you're not for me, you're against me." That's pretty strong. No loopholes there.

Soon after our receiving Jesus as Lord, we visited my father and stepmother in New Jersey. Eagerly I told Dad the whole story, exclamation points and all. He listened intently, but rather sadly, I thought as I studied his face for a response.

Finally he shook his head. "Ceil," he began, his blue eyes intent on mine, "I'm glad for you and Hugh that you have had this experience. I can see it has been good for you. Your joy is evident. But for me . . . " He cleared his throat. Tenderness and regret were in his eyes. "I just can't believe. You see, I am an atheist! "

His words shocked me. He'd never before come out so frankly. His attitude toward God seemed passive, sort of "you go your way, I'll go mine."

I swallowed, tears blurred my sight.

"I'm sorry, dear, but I just can't . . . "

"It's all right, Dad." How I loved him for his honesty and for never trying to pull me back from my faith. He gave me complete freedom in spite of his feelings.

I hugged him and never tried to push my faith on him, though I prayed continually that he would see God's love and believe God for himself.

Some ten years later, Dad had suffered a stroke, gamely limped down the aisle at Gail's wedding, comforted me with beautiful letters while I lay in pain following my spinal fusion. Though our ways of belief differed, love bound us. Not love spoken but felt: a fragrant bouquet of rain-spattered freesia from Dad to me in the hospital, a warm hooded jacket at camp. These were Dad's way of saying, "I care."

Dad suffered from Parkinson's disease. Eventually paralysis in his throat made swallowing difficult. A vigilant nurse restored breathing once, but two days later Dad died. I arrived just in time for the funeral. Deep in his silken coffin, Dad looked peaceful. The service began. The minister's first words hit me. "Jesus said, 'I am the way, the truth, and the life: no man cometh unto the Father, but by me'" (John 14:6). I swallowed hard. "Oh, dear Dad, you denied Jesus. I want that 'way' for you with all my heart. I want to meet you in heaven. Did you ever change your mind?"

The minister continued on with words as evangelical as any I had ever heard. I looked around at my relatives. No reaction on their faces, just quiet listening. I looked over at Dad. He slept on.

"Dad, do you mind?" I wanted to say. "Is this an affront to you? You allowed me to believe. Should I stop this? No, Dad, you never stopped us. It can't hurt you now and someone here may choose God's way today."

All the way home on the plane, I grieved and wondered. To lose someone you love and not know if there will be a reunion in heaven—is any experience more difficult?

Years passed. My sorrow for Dad didn't weaken or die. And God saw my sadness. If I had listened hard enough, perhaps God would have told me, "Your faith is too shallow, Ceil. Hold on, I have a surprise for you."

And God did, a shocking, glory-filled surprise.

In August, just a month after Bill's death, our whole family, including granddaughters Laurie and Linda plus Bill's youngest son, Brad, gathered at Cross Lake.

After a day of strenuous water activity, we ate a hearty dinner. "Phone for you, Ceil," our neighbor yelled from the

outside phone box across from our cabin. I rushed to
answer, wondering who could be calling us there.

"Hi, Ceil. It's Karen. I have some surprising news from
your father."

"Dad? I don't understand. How . . ."

"Well, I finally tackled the job of checking through Bill's
things. I was cleaning out Bill's desk. You know, that
antique one that was your dad's."

"Yes, in your bedroom."

"I emptied the drawer and was scrubbing it when I
discovered a secret compartment. Inside was a neat stack of
papers, all in your father's handwriting."

"Yes, go on."

"On top was a sort of prayer poem that stunned all of us. I
want to read it to you."

Karen read, "Dear God, I know that now my time is
running out fast, that every sunrise or sunset may be my
last. That's why I get up early to see what dawn will bring,
each day a new adventure, each day the start of spring. I
know no other season for all the year around. No matter
what the weather, thy blessings still abound. I'd like to
thank you, God, for all of this. I've been a very ordinary
man, but I've been blessed, through your goodness, with a
very wonderful wife and with children whose love and
accomplishments have made me feel that my life has not
been in vain. Please watch over and guide them that their
lives and my dear grandchildren's lives may follow the
teachings of Jesus Christ. In that hope and faith, I shall enter
the new life."

Tears of joy streamed down my face.

"Are you OK, Ceil?"

"Oh, yes, it's so beautiful and unexpected. Dad wants *us*
to follow Jesus? Oh, Karen, how could he change like this
and not tell anyone?"

"I don't know, but you know your dad was never one to
share his feelings. But I do think he meant for us to find
this."

"Thank you, Karen, dear. No gift could be more precious than this letter from Dad. It's like a message from heaven."

As Brad talked with Karen, I stared at the flaming sunset over the lake. "Every sunset may be my last." *Heaven must be filled with even more beauty than our sunsets and sunrises,* I thought.

There was one time when Dad had told me of his love, but that too was after his death, in his will. He named various bequests, then stated that because he felt Hugh had ample material resources to provide for me, he left me nothing monetary, just his love. The others wondered if that didn't hurt me, but I felt thrilled that Dad had finally said what I had longed to hear for years, "To Ceil I leave my love."

Well, now I had still more, Dad's faith and his admonition, "Follow Jesus."

Calls from God lift us to spiritual heights. What a mysterious and wonderful journey we take as we hurdle hurts and listen to God.

NOTES

1. Paul Tournier, *The Seasons of Life* (Atlanta: John Knox Press, 1976), p. 16.

2. From a lecture, "The Mystery of Suffering," given at Bethel College by Edna Hong, author of *Turn Over Any Stone* (Augsburg, 1970; Tyndale House, 1973).

3. Paul Tournier, *A Place for You* (New York: Harper and Row, 1968), p. 25.

4. The next seven paragraphs are quoted by permission from the author's earlier book, *Another Day, Another Miracle* (Wheaton, Ill.: Tyndale House, 1975), pp. 34, 35.

5. C. S. Lewis, *A Grief Observed* (New York: Bantam, 1976), pp. 55, 69, 72.